D0290440

Praise for
Rise of the Servant Kings

"I have passed the Promise Keepers baton to Ken Harrison with exceeding joy because Ken is a man of the Word and a man of prayer. Never has there been a greater need for men of the Word and prayer because men lead based on who they are. Additionally, Ken has a genuine love for brothers of color and is committed to ensure they are reached, included, and fully involved as Promise Keepers builds an army of godly men. Read this book; it was written by a man of integrity."

—BILL MCCARTNEY, founder of Promise Keepers and former head
football coach at the University of Colorado

"No one will ever accuse Ken Harrison, a gritty ex-policeman who now heads Promise Keepers, of pulling any punches in describing the role of a servant king. His message is clear, direct, and on target as he challenges men to accept their responsibility as Christ followers in all arenas of life. Men of all ages will be encouraged by this timely reminder of both the cost and opportunity of authentic manhood."

—MARK BATTERSON, *New York Times* best-selling author of *The
Circle Maker* and lead pastor of National Community Church

"In *Rise of the Servant Kings*, Ken Harrison explains clearly what the core qualities of a man of God should be. Since Ken is an ex–police officer, he is not afraid to get right to the nitty-gritty in describing how a man can apply the Bible's principles for authentic masculinity in every area of life—from personal integrity to marriage to fatherhood to serving his fellow man. If you want a no-nonsense guide to getting manhood right, this is it."

—EVANDER HOLYFIELD, four-time world heavyweight champion

"Some authors write with ink and some with water. Harrison writes with blood and fire, and his soul-stirring call for men to rise to the challenge of the hour is bold, timely, and heartwarming. If Christian men respond as the promise keepers described here, the world will be a different and better place."

—Os Guinness, author of *The Call: Finding and Fulfilling God's Purpose for Your Life*

"Because I'm a woman, I don't usually read books about being a man, but my husband was reading Ken's book and was so enthusiastic that I wanted to know what set this book apart. Ken's stories captivated me. His honesty inspired me. The book pulses with masculinity, yet God spoke to me, a woman! I'm buying *Rise of the Servant Kings* for every man in my life!"

—Linda Dillow, author of *Intimate Issues, Calm My Anxious Heart,* and other books

"Masculinity, as God designed it, isn't toxic. Rather, it's good, life giving, courageous, and sacrificial. There were times while reading this book when I felt as if Ken were in my face! It was uncomfortable, but what he says is spot-on. I know Ken loves Christ, cares about the right things, and is passionate about seeing God's kingdom advance. The truth he speaks is truth men need to hear."

—John Stonestreet, president of the Colson Center and coauthor of *A Practical Guide to Culture*

"Ken has captured the biblical mandate of manhood. In a world of putting self first, he encourages men to be servant leaders both to their fellow man and to their God."

—Lt. Gen. (Ret.) William G. Boykin, US Army

"Scripture teaches and history affirms that our greatest kings and leaders have strong and loving hearts that beat to serve God, their families, and humanity. Ken writes and leads by example."

—Alveda King, evangelist, author, and activist at www.alvedaking.com

"You may have heard the statement that 'being male is a matter of birth, but being a man is a matter of choice.' Ken Harrison challenges us to the next level, that being a man of God means choosing to live proactively, courageously, and humbly. Masterfully blending deep theological insight with fascinating experiences as part of the LAPD, Ken addresses with sledgehammer force the key issues men struggle with. This book will arrest your heart to choose living out your true design as a servant king!"

—ALAN PLATT, leader of Doxa Deo and City Changers Global

"Ken Harrison is the kind of person he writes about. He's a man of character and conviction, and much of his book calls us to a similar path. I'm thankful that *Rise of the Servant Kings* will encourage men to be who God has called them to be."

—ED STETZER, executive director of the Billy Graham Center
        and dean of the School of Mission, Ministry, and Leadership
        at Wheaton College

"There are many voices speaking to us of manhood today. Ken Harrison's is unique among them. It sounds forth from his gritty years as an LA cop, his inspiring business experience, and his hard-won victories as a leader of men. He is streetwise and biblical, humorous and learned. He issues a call to righteous manhood that we need to hear."

—STEPHEN MANSFIELD, *New York Times* best-selling author

"Little boys don't want to grow up to be polite citizens who keep their lawn manicured. They want to be heroes and even superheroes who right wrongs, deliver the oppressed, and save the world. In *Rise of the Servant Kings,* Ken has done grown-up boys a favor by providing them both a reminder and a road map to experience the true greatness their Father King has planned for them."

—TODD WAGNER, author of *Come and See* and founding pastor
        of Watermark Community Church

RISE OF THE SERVANT KINGS

FOREWORD BY STU WEBER

RISE OF THE SERVANT KINGS

WHAT THE BIBLE SAYS
ABOUT BEING A MAN

KEN HARRISON

Chairman of the Board, Promise Keepers

MULTNOMAH

RISE OF THE SERVANT KINGS

All Scripture quotations, unless otherwise indicated, are taken from the Holman Christian Standard Bible®, copyright © 1999, 2000, 2002, 2003, 2009 by Holman Bible Publishers. Used by permission. HCSB® is a federally registered trademark of Holman Bible Publishers. Scripture quotations marked (NIV) are taken from the Holy Bible, New International Version®, NIV®. Copyright © 1973, 1978, 1984, 2011 by Biblica Inc.® Used by permission. All rights reserved worldwide.

Details in some anecdotes and stories have been changed to protect the identities of the persons involved.

Hardcover ISBN 978-0-525-65318-9
eBook ISBN 978-0-525-65319-6

Copyright © 2019 by Ken Harrison

Cover design by Mark D. Ford; photography by Magdalena Russocka/Trevillion Images

All rights reserved. No part of this book may be reproduced or transmitted in any form or by any means, electronic or mechanical, including photocopying and recording, or by any information storage and retrieval system, without permission in writing from the publisher.

Published in the United States by Multnomah, an imprint of the Crown Publishing Group, a division of Penguin Random House LLC, New York.

MULTNOMAH® and its mountain colophon are registered trademarks of Penguin Random House LLC.

Library of Congress Cataloging-in-Publication Data
Names: Harrison, K. R. (Ken R.), author.
Title: Rise of the servant kings : what the Bible says about being a man / by Ken Harrison.
Description: First Edition. | Colorado Springs : Multnomah, 2019.
Identifiers: LCCN 2018036965 | ISBN 9780525653189 (hardcover) | ISBN 9780525653196 (electronic)
Subjects: LCSH: Christian men—Religious life—Biblical teaching. | Men (Christian theology)
Classification: LCC BV4528.2 .H364 2019 | DDC 248.8/42—dc23
LC record available at https://lccn.loc.gov/2018036965

Printed in the United States of America
2019—First Edition

10 9 8 7 6 5 4 3 2 1

SPECIAL SALES
Most Multnomah books are available at special quantity discounts when purchased in bulk by corporations, organizations, and special-interest groups. Custom imprinting or excerpting can also be done to fit special needs. For information, please email specialmarketscms@penguinrandomhouse.com or call 1-800-603-7051.

To Elliette—my best friend,
my fellow prayer warrior, my servant queen

Contents

Foreword

Some tell me there are only three things in this world that last forever—people, principles, and stories. And most of the stories are about people learning principles. *Rise of the Servant Kings* draws on events from a man's story and shares the principles he has learned along the way. Some the hard way.

This book reveals pieces of Ken's story, so you'll encounter plenty of rough edges in these pages. Some of your feathers may get ruffled. Ken writes like the tough LAPD street cop he once was—direct, forceful, staccato, no nonsense. Just rapid-fire bursts of truth intended to hit your center of mass with intensity and energy. But don't miss the point. There is hope here. This man from Boring, Oregon, whom I've known since he was a young "holy terror," is on another mission that's not so boring. This mission is from heaven.

Ken's mission matters like no other has in his life. Though he is a successful businessman, this mission is not about money or competition. Not about personal achievement. No mere earthly pettiness. This mission is about a singular cause that transcends all else—the kingdom of Christ ruling in every masculine soul to the end that men actually become mature in Christ, marriages reflect heaven, families become healthy, communities are revolutionized, and, above all else, our God is glorified.

When Jesus conquers a man and that man surrenders fully to Him, everyone within range benefits and rejoices. His wife, kids, friends, neighbors, church, even his whole community—everyone wins! God loves to use converted, humbled Christ-following men. He has a way of growing them up.

Come along and profit from principles Ken has learned in his life. Hang on for the ride; ponder the white spaces. And read this book with the burden from which it was written: This earth is not the real world. One day, at the end of the race, you and every believer will stand before the King for His evaluation.

Join the rise of the servant kings!

—Stu Weber, pastor, speaker, and author of *Tender Warrior*

RISE OF THE SERVANT KINGS

Chapter 1

SERVANT KINGS

I looked for pleasure, beauty, and truth not in Him but in myself and His other creatures, and the search led me instead to pain, confusion, and error.

—AUGUSTINE, *Confessions*

Don't you know that the runners in a stadium all race, but only one receives the prize? Run in such a way to win the prize. Now everyone who competes exercises self-control in everything. However, they do it to receive a crown that will fade away, but we a crown that will never fade away. Therefore I do not run like one who runs aimlessly or box like one beating the air. Instead, I discipline my body and bring it under strict control, so that after preaching to others, I myself will not be disqualified.

—1 CORINTHIANS 9:24–27

T he athlete stood and stretched, the sound of the warning trumpet still filling his ears. The sun wasn't yet up, and the cold of the January morning filled his bones. He watched his breath trail into the air and shivered as his trainer rubbed him with oil, getting his blood flowing. A slave fed him cheese, figs, and dried meats, the only food he'd have for months. He stomped his feet impatiently, knowing that if he missed the next trumpet, he'd be disqualified from the greatest moment of his life. Despite the cold, there was no need to dress. He'd train today naked, the same way he'd compete.

The athlete had been selected to represent his city in the Isthmian Games, and he'd met every qualification. He was a freeborn Greek, he'd won the qualifying matches, and he'd met the standards set by the city elders. Now came the real challenge. He would train every day for ten months, his every move monitored by the marshals. If any of them thought he was giving less than maximum effort, for even an instant, he would be cast out. If he ever left the training grounds, he would be disqualified. If wine or any food beyond the approved diet touched his lips, he would be sent home with deep shame, with "weeping and gnashing of teeth."

The training was grueling, and there were no breaks. And no mercy. He represented the people of his city and served at their discretion. The effort was worth it. If he won, he'd be a ceremonial king, given the crown of Poseidon and the glory that went with it. The city would shower him with rewards. The people would honor him with a parade and write songs about him. A ceremonial hole would be cut in the city wall to symbolize that with such a great athlete, the people didn't need walls to protect them from their enemies— they had him. His family would be fed and would be forgiven from taxes for his lifetime, and his children would go to the best academy. Even better, he would be given a lifetime appointment to the city council.[1] If only he could stay focused during his time at the training grounds and not be disqualified from the race. He thought, *I must "discipline my body and bring it under strict control, so that . . . I myself will not be disqualified."*

This is the athlete Paul had in mind as he wrote the verses at the beginning of this chapter. This is the only type of athlete the Corinthians would recognize—a man who had mastered self-control and was focused so completely on victory that if he ran the race well, the city officials would lavish awards on him.

Here Paul gave us the template for our Christian walk. We are to run the race of life to win the crown and the rewards and recognition that come with it. Paul put the message of Christ—that all who have believed in Him have been selected to represent Him in the game of life—into terms the Greeks could relate to, ideas like these:

- We are the freeborn (we were born in bondage to sin; when we became born again, we were freed from our bondage to sin). We were selected from the very beginning of time (Ephesians 1:4).
- Some of us will receive the crown of victory at the judgment of the Christians (1 Peter 5:4; 2 Timothy 4:8), and some of us will hang our heads in shame (1 Corinthians 3:13–15; 1 John 2:28) because we have not run the race to win.
- If we don't stay focused on victory, there will be consequences for our actions on earth and consequences in heaven. All our experiences in life have taught us that we reap what we sow (Galatians 6:7).

An Obedient Life

When I was nineteen, I got a job at an underage nightclub working as a door-man. I had walked with the Lord my whole life, so this job was getting me an education in a world with which I was completely unfamiliar. The club was in a rough area of town, and homeless people often milled around the front door. There was one homeless man who was like a mirror image of me, only black. He was the same age, height, and build and always seemed to be around. Even on warm summer days, he was never without his denim jacket with brown corduroy sleeves.

I'd often go to a sandwich place that was open late to get something to eat. Sometimes I ate only half the sandwich and gave the other half to him. I didn't think much about it; he was hungry and I had half a sandwich. On a few cold nights I bought him coffee. Each time I handed him something, he'd just nod. I never heard him say a word.

I really didn't fit in with the scene at that club, and my Christian lifestyle and values were apparent to the owners. They never saw me take part in the club's activities, so, regarding me as a trustworthy employee, they promoted me to manager within a few months.

One night three guys in their late teens forced their way through the front door without paying admission, and I was called on to confront them. Some-how I got them outside the door, but as we exited, one of the teens threw a punch that caught me square on my jaw. He hit me again and then again. He hit me about ten times over the next thirty seconds. He was a trained fighter and moved and punched far more quickly than I could defend myself. I was finally able to get ahold of him and got him to the ground, which ended the fight. I looked around, wondering what had happened to the other two teens and saw them stretched out on the ground, unconscious. Standing over them was the homeless man, fists clenched. He was barely breathing hard.

"Thanks, man," was all I could say between gasps for breath. He just nodded.

Twenty years later, after becoming the CEO of a large company, I was walking down the sidewalk in the same city when I saw that homeless man. I could hardly believe it—he was wearing the same denim jacket with the corduroy sleeves. It was tattered and dirty but the same jacket. I emptied my wallet and walked up to him, handing him the cash. "You helped me out once," I said. He just nodded and walked away.

This was similar to an event that happened to an officer I knew while I was a police officer with the Los Angeles Police Department (LAPD). We were working in the notoriously high-crime area called 77th Division. The gang war was in full swing, and we were struggling with a vicious gang called the Eight Trey Crips. Though they were part of the Crips street gang, they killed other Crips, as well as those from their rival gang, the Bloods.

Around two o'clock in the morning on a hot summer night, I was writing an arrest report in the break room of 77th station. An officer walked in with a dazed look in his eyes and a bandage on his head. He shuffled over to the coffee dispenser and put a quarter in, waiting for the weak, lukewarm coffee to drip into a tiny cup. Then he threw down a sheet of paper and stared at it, trying to figure out how to start a report. "Man, what happened to you?" I asked.

He blinked and focused slowly on my face. Looking back on it, I realize now that he probably had a concussion, but in those days we were told to "just shake it off."

"I was in a foot pursuit of a couple of Eight Treys, man," the officer said. "I got separated from my partner during the pursuit and jumped over a fence. The kid I was chasing ducked under a clothesline, and when I went to tackle him, the line got me under the chin. I never saw it. It flipped me backward, and I bounced my head off the concrete. Knocked me out cold, man."

He blinked a few times. "I woke up indoors on some guy's couch. He'd seen the whole thing, come outside, and carried me into his house and hid me from the Crips." The officer held his head in his hands, trying to quell the pain.

"They'll kill him for that," I said.

"Yeah . . . no," he said, furrowing his brow. "We called the fire department, and they snuck me out of his house on a stretcher. The gangsters didn't see he had a cop in his house." He shook his head slowly. "When I came to, the guy said, 'I seen you around before. You were always fair to everyone. You're one of the good cops. I wasn't gonna let them kill you.' You know, Harrison, if those Eight Treys would've seen me laying there unconscious, they'd have put a bullet in my head."

"Yeah," I said, "you got lucky."

"No," he said, "I treat everyone with respect. I never figured people were watching though. I never thought it would save my life."

His actions had consequences, and they saved his life. My actions as a teenager had consequences, and they saved me a trip to the emergency room. In his case and mine, black men risked their safety and even their lives to save white men because of some small acts of kindness that neither of us realized would come to matter so much.

Giving a cup of coffee to a cold man, treating poor people with respect, these are small actions that should typify every Christian (Matthew 10:42). But they don't typify every Christian, do they? These are not actions that can simply be summoned up when you want them. They are consequences of living a life of obedience to God.

A man who is in love with God is a man who is in love with other people. Neither that fellow officer nor I thought about what we were doing. Our actions were the outward expression of our nature. We were men in love with Jesus. We acted like servant kings.

Let's Talk

Let's have a truly honest discussion about what the Bible says about God's plan for men.

God wants us to be His servant kings.

What does that look like? A real man is proactive, courageous, and humble, but our sinful nature pulls us toward passivity, cowardice, and arrogance. Our sinful nature says to us, "As soon as you get your act together, then you can try to be and do something meaningful."

That's a lie. God seeks men of action and faith who will "go before they know."

In this book we don't want to gain more facts about God. We want to come to know God Himself. We've been invited into relationship with Him, so let's get to know Him and what He wants from us. Let's also take an honest look at why it's so hard to draw close to Him despite His invitation. We want to learn how to have true life as we step out in bold obedience and trust in His Word.

Well Done!

How would you complete the following sentence? The goal of my life is

_____.

The goal of football is to score touchdowns. The goal of running a company is to increase profits or stock value. What's the goal of your life? Let's take a look at a crucial Bible passage and see if we can come up with an answer:

> It is just like a man going on a journey. He called his own slaves and turned over his possessions to them. To one he gave five talents; to another, two; and to another, one—to each according to his own ability. Then he went on a journey. Immediately the man who had received five talents went, put them to work, and earned five more. In the same way the man with two earned two more. But the man who had received one talent went off, dug a hole in the ground, and hid his master's money.
>
> After a long time the master of those slaves came and settled accounts with them. The man who had received five talents approached, presented five more talents, and said, "Master, you gave me five talents. Look, I've earned five more talents."

His master said to him, "Well done, good and faithful slave! You were faithful over a few things; I will put you in charge of many things. Share your master's joy!"

Then the man with two talents also approached. He said, "Master, you gave me two talents. Look, I've earned two more talents."

His master said to him, "Well done, good and faithful slave! You were faithful over a few things; I will put you in charge of many things. Share your master's joy!"

Then the man who had received one talent also approached and said, "Master, I know you. You're a difficult man, reaping where you haven't sown and gathering where you haven't scattered seed. So I was afraid and went off and hid your talent in the ground. Look, you have what is yours."

But his master replied to him, "You evil, lazy slave! If you knew that I reap where I haven't sown and gather where I haven't scattered, then you should have deposited my money with the bankers. And when I returned I would have received my money back with interest.

"So take the talent from him and give it to the one who has 10 talents. For to everyone who has, more will be given, and he will have more than enough. But from the one who does not have, even what he has will be taken away from him. And throw this good-for-nothing slave into the outer darkness. In that place there will be weeping and gnashing of teeth." (Matthew 25:14–30)

A man with a goal in life is active because he knows what he's pursuing. Let's live lives that the Savior deems "Well done!"

God delights in communicating Himself and His ways to every man who is prepared to receive Him. God can work in you only to the extent that you are submitted to Him. We all have some "self" left in us. Every believer is granted the Holy Spirit the moment he receives Christ (Ephesians 1:13–14). The amount of influence the Spirit has on you depends on the extent of your surrender: *the more self, the less God; the less self, the more God.*

When I was with the LAPD and arrested someone, sometimes I was present when the jailer fingerprinted the prisoner. He would roll each finger in ink and then roll it onto the page. The jailer needed the finger absolutely yielded to him to get a good print. If there were any smudges, he would have to throw the card out and start over.

Often the prisoner would try to help and would smudge the print. The jailer would get angry and order him to relax every muscle and trust the jailer to do all the work. Some prisoners were unable to simply yield, and the process took a long time compared with those who yielded and completed the process easily.

That's a picture of how God wants to work with us—life goes better when we relax and let Him work through us. He's patient, willing to work on us throughout our entire lives, teaching us to yield to Him. But we have to let Him do it. Self wants to help; self wants to get credit. It chafes at the idea that God will do all and self can do nothing—except *yield*.

In our efforts to "help," we have smudged the edges, putting the ugly print of human pride and self-effort where only our Lord should have received the glory. Jesus said that for us to enter the kingdom of heaven, we must be like little children (Matthew 18:3). He meant that our surrender must be one of simple, childlike trust in our Father. He will accept our surrender and fill us with His great power and fellowship.

Preseason Football

Too many men today are doing life as if it's a preseason football game. We think that because we've received Christ and can't lose our salvation, there is nothing left but to seek our own pleasures and obey some set of rules that someone somewhere told us. We do the best we can, but it really doesn't count, does it?

No one likes preseason football. God has told us to snatch people from the hands of Satan and bring them into His loving arms. He's told us to protect and provide for His children and to care for the less fortunate. Life is the playoffs, not the preseason.

And when the game's over, we get only one shot to hear Jesus say, "Well done, my son!" So let us do the work that God gave us and, with it, experience the joy and reward of serving our Lord.

God knows that it is hard for us to obey and to have a nature that treats others respectfully and kindly. He knows that we yearn like little children to please our Father but fail over and over. That is why He urges us through the apostle Paul's writing to stay intensely focused, just like a Corinthian athlete. He will always meet us where we are if our hearts are pure. He will lift us to victory, but it will often be difficult.

In the next few chapters we will dig into why it is so hard to become the men we so desperately want to be. We will learn how to become servant kings.

Chapter 2

THE FALL

Our problem is not that we're human; it's that we're fallen.

> —JOHN STONESTREET, cohost of
> BreakPoint Radio

Therefore, just as sin entered the world through one man, and death through sin, in this way death spread to all men, because all sinned.

> —ROMANS 5:12

Have you ever held a young person in your arms and watched her die? There is something about it that stays with a man until he takes his last breath.

When I was a Los Angeles police officer, my partner and I would often sneak out of our division into neighboring divisions where we could get something decent to eat for Code 7 (lunch). There wasn't much to eat in the ghetto at two o'clock in the morning, so we often drove north to the USC campus or the Hollywood area. Code 7 was forty-five minutes of peace amid the chaos.

My partner and I were eating late-night pancakes when a hysterical woman ran into the restaurant, screaming that there had been a car crash just outside and people were dying. It sounds harsh, but at the time we resented being bothered. This was supposed to be our moment of peace, and we saw dying people all the time. We radioed for an RA unit (paramedics) and some officers from Traffic Division to handle the accident and walked outside.

You just never know what is around the corner or just outside Denny's. A motorcycle was down, crushed under a car. A boy about eighteen was unconscious, bleeding severely from his head. He wasn't wearing a helmet. Behind him on the bike was a beautiful girl, also about eighteen. She had a helmet, and I didn't see any blood on her. But her eyes had the glassy stare of the dying.

She looked up at me and put her arms out like a child wanting a hug. I stood there, thinking about what had been drilled into me through training—*never touch a wounded person unless there's a life-saving need.*

"Hold me," she whispered. It was a plea. So I sat down and wrapped my arms around her, putting her head in my lap.

The boy woke up and looked at us, unmoving.

"I was taking her to the hospital," he said. "Her brother was just in a motorcycle accident. I wanted to get her there as fast as possible. Man, what did I do? Is she going to live?"

Then she convulsed. Her body shuddered with the seizure of the dying. I held her closer and tried to calm her body. It seemed disgraceful to let her spasm like that. I think I was trying to hold her soul in, to keep her from dying there on the street.

Her convulsions slowed, and as I was watching her face, she looked up, but not at my face. Her eyes were on my badge. She kept moving her lips, trying to speak, but no sounds came out. She reached up and grasped my badge, and then the life left her eyes. One moment I was holding life in my arms. The next I was holding a corpse. She was gone.

The two traffic cops we'd requested showed up on their motorcycles. It was the same two older officers who seemed to show up every time I needed a traffic unit. There was a strange sort of camaraderie between us, even though we had barely spoken to one another, maybe because we'd handled so many horrific accidents together.

I was hesitant to speak because I was afraid I'd cry. "He was taking her to the hospital to see her brother," I blurted out. "The brother was just in a motorcycle accident."

The traffic cops looked at each other and then back at me. "Hollywood Presbyterian?" one of them asked.

I nodded.

"Oh no!" the other said. "We just came from handling that accident. Her brother died."

We all just stood there for a moment, looking at her. "You know the thing about it, man?" one of them said. "Their parents are on vacation. These were their only two kids."

The Problem

When I watched this girl die in my arms, it hit me particularly hard because it was one of the few times I'd watched an innocent person die. I'd seen criminals die many times, and that hurt less. Watching someone die is always the same—there is a distinctly visual sense of the soul leaving the body.

When we see the tragedy of death right in front of us, it seems unnatural. But everyone must die, so if we are just a collection of cells, death should seem just a mundane part of human existence, right? Instead, death is a horrifyingly terrible moment, and it genuinely feels wrong when it happens.

It's strange that we all have such a deep conviction that death isn't the end, unless, of course, it isn't the end at all. The Bible teaches us that our souls are eternal and death is our separation from the bodies in which they are housed. But what happens to our souls when our bodies die, and why is that separation so terrifying?

I'll answer that question, but let's first look at what evil is and why it exists. Knowing that helps us understand death and its hold on us.

What Is Evil?

When God created human beings, He gave us freedom of choice. The choice was between life and knowledge. In the Garden of Eden, Adam and Eve could have eaten from the tree of life but chose instead the tree of the knowledge of good and evil (Genesis 3:1–7). Life would have consisted of an eternity living in God's presence and learning more and more of His nature. But when human beings chose knowledge over life, we entered the realm of death. The desire to know became our greatest temptation; it became more valuable than obedience or even life. This is why faith is so integral to knowing God. Faith is the first step away from the need to know and toward true life.

Death, like evil or darkness, is not a thing; rather, it is the lack of a thing. It is a parasite, deriving its essence from something else. Darkness wasn't created; it is simply a lack of light. In the same way, cold is the absence of heat. If you grasp a cold door handle, you aren't feeling cold; you're feeling the door handle robbing you of the heat from your hand.

In this way, death and evil are really the same thing; they are both not God. People who do not understand God claim that if He created everything, He must have created evil. No. When God created a person with a choice, the potential for evil was born. Once that someone chose something other than God, evil became reality, and with it came death—because God is life (John 11:25; John 14:6; 1 John 5:20).

The terror of death is on us all because as long as we're trapped in our shells—our bodies—we most often seek to operate in the known. We operate in the place in which our sinful nature is most comfortable—the place of knowledge. Separation from our bodies brings us outside the realm of our control. And that reality will be a place devoid of the light and life of God for those who die in their sins: "It is a terrifying thing to fall into the hands of the living God!" (Hebrews 10:31). On the other hand, for those who have received the redemption of Jesus Christ, "entry into the eternal kingdom of our Lord and Savior Jesus Christ will be richly supplied" (2 Peter 1:11).

At the moment of death, those who have had their sins forgiven by Jesus Christ will find that having their souls separated from their bodies will be a moment of peace, not terror. One of C. S. Lewis's friends, upon seeing him the day before he died in 1963, said that he had never seen a person so prepared to die.[2]

What Are We?

"God said, 'Let Us make man in Our image, according to Our likeness. They will rule the fish of the sea, the birds of the sky, the livestock, all the earth, and the creatures that crawl on the earth'" (Genesis 1:26). Most Christians seem to start to build their understanding of theology in Genesis 3, which documents the curse, instead of starting in Genesis 1. We were created in God's image and therefore yearn to do good, but we behave badly anyway due to our fallen nature. We all are evil and need the salvation of Christ (Romans 3:23). What makes us so bad is that because we were created in God's image, we know better. We inherently know what is right and desire it, but we do the opposite anyway. When God created human beings, He called them "very good" (Genesis 1:31). God created us to rule the earth and fill it. He rested on the seventh day, not because the work was done, but because He was giving us the responsibility to shepherd every living thing as life spread, each according to its kind, throughout the earth (Genesis 1:28). So what went wrong?

George MacDonald is quoted as saying, "Never tell a child, you *have* a soul. Teach him, you *are* a soul; you have a body."[3] I believe this is why the young woman I held on the street that night felt so different after she had died. She had left.

A proper view of our bodies is necessary for us to understand the Fall and God's warnings about living "according to the flesh" (Romans 8:4–5, 12–13). Andrew Murray wrote,

> When God created man a living soul, that soul, as the seat and
> organ of his personality and consciousness, was linked on the one
> side, through the body, with the outer visible world, and on the
> other side, through the spirit, with the unseen and the divine. The
> soul had to decide whether it would yield itself to the spirit and by it
> to be linked with God and His will, or to the body and the solicita-
> tions of the visible. In the fall, the soul refused the rule of the spirit
> and became the slave of the body with its earthly appetites.[4]

Humans were created to worship. When we chose something other than God in the garden, evil became not only our reality but also our nature, and our fellowship with Him was broken. Just as Adam and Eve hid from God in the garden because of their shame, we naturally hide from Him too. But still we seek to worship, so we worship self.

With this perspective we begin to understand 1 Corinthians 2:14: "The unbeliever does not welcome what comes from God's Spirit, because it is foolishness to him; he is not able to understand it since it is evaluated spiritually." We naturally evaluate things from the perspective of our flesh, which is not of God.

The corrupted soul sometimes looks to its own thoughts and feelings and tries to find goodness and peace. This is the ego and is encouraged by the ways of the world, which say, "Look inside and you will find the answer." Our Creator has a different perspective: "The heart is more deceitful than anything else, and incurable—who can understand it?" (Jeremiah 17:9). There is nothing inside but self, demanding to be worshipped.

You may be thinking that people don't often worship themselves— more often they hate themselves. However, self-loathing always derives from self-obsession. Have you ever known a person who lives completely to serve others? Have you noticed how that person is always filled with joy? The opposite is true as well. A person who focuses on self is always miserable. A depressed or suicidal person obsesses over self to the point of utter misery. Let's look at why.

The Curse

The creation eagerly waits with anticipation for God's sons to be revealed. For the creation was subjected to futility—not willingly, but because of Him who subjected it—in the hope that the creation itself will also be set free from the bondage of corruption into the glorious freedom of God's children. For we know that the whole creation has been groaning together with labor pains until now. And not only that, but we ourselves who have the Spirit as the firstfruits—we also groan within ourselves, eagerly waiting for adoption, the redemption of our bodies. Now in this hope we were saved, yet hope that is seen is not hope, because who hopes for what he sees? But if we hope for what we do not see, we eagerly wait for it with patience. (Romans 8:19–25)

All of nature fell under a curse because of the sin of human beings. When God announced the curses on mankind and nature in Genesis 3, He was not doling out punishment. He was declaring the consequences of sin. If my son drives drunk and crashes his car, breaking his leg, and I say, "Now you're going to miss the wrestling season," I'm not punishing him. Rather, I'm simply explaining the consequences of his actions.

It is interesting to note that God gave three aspects of life to people *before* the Fall: food, work, and sex. Mankind was to eat of the garden, work the garden, and be fruitful and multiply (1:28–29; 2:15). Notice that these are also the three aspects of life that received the curse (3:16–19). One of the most beautiful outcomes of sex is children, which now come through a mother's hard labor. The harvest of our food comes through labor (in fact, the same Hebrew word for *labor* is used to refer to childbirth and farming), and toil will no longer be a constant reward but a daily fight.

When God told Adam and Eve not to eat from the forbidden tree, He warned them that they would "certainly die" (2:17). After God declared the consequences of their sin, He gave Adam and Eve skins to wear, covering their shame. God was no longer creating, which means He had to kill an animal to get the skin to cover their shame. Can you imagine the horrific moment for Adam and Eve, who had never known death, to see an animal in their care killed because of their actions? This also foreshadowed what must eventually take place: someday an ultimate death would be required to cover the sin of all men.

Consequences

> I know that nothing good lives in me, that is, in my flesh. For the desire to do what is good is with me, but there is no ability to do it. For I do not do the good that I want to do, but I practice the evil that I do not want to do. . . . For in my inner self I joyfully agree with God's law. But I see a different law in the parts of my body, waging war against the law of my mind and taking me prisoner to the law of sin in the parts of my body. What a wretched man I am! Who will rescue me from this dying body? I thank God through Jesus Christ our Lord! So then, with my mind I myself am a slave to the law of God, but with my flesh, to the law of sin. (Romans 7:18–19, 22–25)

As humans, we deeply want to do good, but we do evil instead. We want to be kind and generous, but something else lurks inside—something that drives us to take and destroy. We fight our own sin nature.

In the Scripture passage above, the apostle Paul wrote of our state of desperation when we make unhealthy choices and also of the relief we feel when we turn to the Savior. Jesus died to free us from this state and sent His Spirit to keep us free. As believers, we no longer are slaves to sin; the victory has been won—our sin nature is dead! We still commit sins, but we no longer are compelled to sin by a sin nature. Sin loses its appeal as we grow in Christ and begin to see the world through His eyes, and fellowship with Him becomes easier and easier.

As we grow as Christians, the Holy Spirit continues to conquer any inclination in us to sin, reminds us of our new nature in Christ, and helps us increasingly become a true reflection of God's image. As we learn to turn from our inclination to sin, the Holy Spirit begins to have greater influence in us. We begin to learn how to become servant kings.

Chapter 3

THE LIAR

We must remember that Satan has his miracles too.

—JOHN CALVIN, *Institutes of the Christian Religion*

If you have bitter envy and selfish ambition in your heart,
don't brag and deny the truth. Such wisdom does not
come from above but is earthly, unspiritual, demonic. For
where envy and selfish ambition exist, there is disorder
and every kind of evil.

—JAMES 3:14–16

I looked into the eyes of Satan once and was terrified. In the summer of 1989 I was touring the Los Angeles County Jail, the largest jail system in the world. I checked my gun into a locker at the entrance and walked into a jail that processes twenty thousand inmates every day.[5] Many of the prisoners are just passing through on their way somewhere else. Some are serving a few days, some are waiting to be processed to a penitentiary, and some really bad ones are there while going through trial.

My uncle was a well-known captain for the LAPD, so the deputies who ran the jail had offered my partner and me a private tour behind the scenes. As we walked down the corridors, the two deputies motioned to hundreds of prisoners all around us. One of them said, "Think about it, man. There are at least five hundred men staring at us right now. Most of 'em want to kill us and we don't even have guns."

I looked around with this comforting thought in mind and wasn't happy. I was even less happy when we rounded a corner and saw a sea of new prisoners waiting to be processed. They were sitting on the floor shoulder to shoulder. The rows were twelve men wide and extended as far down the hall as we could see. There were at least a thousand men waiting, all staring at us with hatred in their eyes.

That was when I saw the biggest man I've ever laid eyes on. He was about six foot six and well over three hundred pounds. His skin was as white as ivory, and his shoulders exploded with muscle. His neck seemed as big as my torso, and his head looked like a giant rock. His eyes were set deep into a thick skull. He wasn't wearing a shirt, and on his chest I saw a giant black swastika tattoo. Over the swastika was a racial slur of violence and hatred.

With the exception of the four officers standing next to him, he was the only white man in the throng of black and brown skin. I asked him, "How do you survive in prison with that tattoo, man?"

He looked at me with dead eyes and answered, "Because I'm the baddest man in here."

We measured each other the way violent men do, and we both knew he could crush me. I knew that if I hit that giant block of granite atop his shoulders with everything I had, he wouldn't move. "You know, I believe you" was all I said as we walked on.

We shuffled toward the solitary-confinement wing, and one of the deputies looked at me and said, "He ain't the baddest dude in here, you know."

"Seriously? He's the scariest man I've ever seen."

The deputies looked at each other and smirked. Every Los Angeles County deputy had to work as a jailer at the Los Angeles County Jail for the first three years of his career, so by the time they got to the streets, they'd seen it all. I was about to learn that the hulking ball of muscle in the hall was only the JV of evil. They kept the varsity in the area we now were walking toward.

We entered the solitary-confinement wing, and they pointed toward several cells, giving us the celebrity tour. "Over there is Todd Bridges, the kid from *Diff'rent Strokes*. He got picked up in a drive-by shooting. He wants to be a gangster, but we have to keep him in here or the real gangsters will rip him to shreds." (For the record, Bridges was later acquitted.) "Over there is one of you guys—LAPD. He got mad at his old lady a couple of nights ago and put nine rounds into her chest. Gotta keep him in here too. If we put him in the general population, he wouldn't last five seconds."

I thought about the three-hundred-pound tattooed giant I'd just met and cringed, thinking about what he'd do if he got his hands on an unarmed LA cop.

"You don't care about them though," one of the deputies said. Then he nodded toward a cell across the room. "Go say hi to the Night Stalker."

He grinned proudly like a zookeeper pointing out a prized baby panda. I looked toward a metal door with a tiny window. The door was set in a steel frame embedded in concrete. I boldly walked to the window and looked inside. When I saw the man inside, my bones turned to jelly.

I was looking into a face of pure evil.

He stood just back from the door and looked deeply into my eyes. He stared at me as if I were an insect, and in his presence I felt like one. He was like a younger, better-looking version of Anthony Hopkins in the film *The Silence of the Lambs,* but Hopkins couldn't begin to capture the sheer evil in Richard Ramirez.

I jumped back from the door, and the deputies laughed. "Everyone does that when they see that freak for the first time, man. Don't worry about it. You get used to it."

Ramirez was in the middle of the trial in which he'd be convicted of thirteen murders. They were only the ones we knew about. He'd broken into houses and slaughtered many men while they slept and then tortured and raped their wives next to their husbands' bodies. He was an avowed Satan worshipper, and apparently the devil had sent his top boys to take full possession of him.[6] When I hear people brag that they cast demons out of people as if it's a small thing, I shake my head. They may have dealt with something evil, but they likely have never encountered what I saw in the face of the Night Stalker. There was a different kind of evil behind his eyes than I had seen before or have seen since.

When my partner and I left the jail, strapping on our gun belts felt much less assuring than usual. Suddenly all the training, weight lifting, and practicing gun skills felt like nothing after seeing Ramirez. *How in the world would we fight an enemy like that?*

Who Is Satan?

We saw in the last chapter that we cannot be successful as followers of Jesus until we understand that we have a wicked nature from which we must turn. We will see in this chapter that we cannot become servant kings until we understand that we have an enemy who works tirelessly to turn us back to that nature.

A king knows who he is and fights with passion to keep his enemy from taking territory. He also fights to protect those in his care from his enemy. Satan hates you, he hates your family, and he hates the church. Let's look at who he is, what he wants, and how to fight him.

Scripture has quite a bit to say about Satan, yet most Christians are ignorant about him. God has written some adamant warnings about our enemy, so let's heed them carefully. Many Christians are under constant attack by him but have no idea of the battle they're in. They think their lack of joy, broken relationships, and failures in life originate with them, when in reality their troubles are because they are following the voice of the enemy of their souls but are completely unaware of it.

Satan is an incredibly powerful angel who became arrogant and wanted to place his throne above God, the one who created him. Here's one biblical description of what happened to Satan:

> Shining morning star,
> how you have fallen from the heavens!
> You destroyer of nations,
> you have been cut down to the ground.
> You said to yourself:
> "I will ascend to the heavens;

I will set up my throne
above the stars of God.
I will sit on the mount of the gods' assembly,
in the remotest parts of the North.
I will ascend above the highest clouds;
I will make myself like the Most High."
But you will be brought down to Sheol [hell]
into the deepest regions of the Pit. (Isaiah 14:12–15)

In another Scripture passage we read this:

You were the seal of perfection,
full of wisdom and perfect in beauty.
You were in Eden, the garden of God.
Every kind of precious stone covered you:
carnelian, topaz, and diamond,
beryl, onyx, and jasper,
sapphire, turquoise and emerald.
Your mountings and settings were crafted in gold;
they were prepared on the day you were created.
You were an anointed guardian cherub,
for I had appointed you.
You were on the holy mountain of God;
you walked among the fiery stones.
From the day you were created
you were blameless in your ways
until wickedness was found in you.
Through the abundance of your trade,
you were filled with violence, and you sinned.
So I expelled you in disgrace
from the mountain of God,

and banished you, guardian cherub,

from among the fiery stones.

Your heart became proud because of your beauty;

For the sake of your splendor

you corrupted your wisdom.

So I threw you down to the earth;

I made you a spectacle before kings. (Ezekiel 28:12–17)

Earlier in the verses from Isaiah, the story is about the king of Babylon, but then the focus switches to describing Satan. Ezekiel 28 starts with a description of the king of Tyre, then similarly switches to describing Satan's downfall. Many prophecies in Scripture contain double meanings. In these two cases, the Lord uses these passages to tell us where Satan came from, while comparing the wickedness and arrogance of these kings to the devil himself. Interestingly, it was the king of Babylon in Isaiah 14 who defeated the king of Tyre described in Ezekiel 28.

We tend to associate fleshly temptation with him by saying things like "The devil made me do it." But Satan has never had human flesh and understands the human experience only from observation. For example, he has no experience of sexual pleasure or what it's like to eat. Satan can tempt us based only on his observations of us. Certainly, he can place things in front of us to tempt us, but when we blame Satan for sins of the flesh, we're making excuses for our own sinful nature, which Jesus pointed out: "You are of your father the Devil, and you want to carry out your father's desires. He was a murderer from the beginning and has not stood in the truth, because there is no truth in him. When he tells a lie, he speaks from his own nature, because he is a liar and the father of liars" (John 8:44).

Satan is a liar and murderer. This part of him comes from his true nature, which, according to the passages quoted above, consists of arrogance, vanity, envy, and selfish ambition. When we act in such a manner, we align ourselves with Satan as enemies of God. This is why the mark of a man of God is humility and absolute surrender to our Lord.

Paul got to the essence of this idea in Philippians 2:3, where he wrote, "Do nothing out of rivalry or conceit, but in humility consider others as more important than yourselves."

What Does Satan Want?

What about the following scenario sounds familiar? Imagine you hated Someone with everything in your being. Imagine that you hated Him so much that you built your entire existence around the goal of hurting Him. Now imagine that He is perfect and untouchable. The Object of your hatred is so far above you that you can never reach Him, let alone hurt Him . . . but you *can* get to His children.

Laying aside any moral sense you have or any restraint, what might you do? If you said that you'd kill His children, you need to try harder. If you could get His children to fight and kill one another or even kill themselves, wouldn't that be the best revenge? And in the process, if you could get His children to hate their Father, wouldn't that be even better? Now, if you could get them to kill one another based on a warped idea of what their Father wanted, so that they actually thought they were killing one another as a way of fixing their failed relationship with Him, then that would be the ultimate revenge, right?

And how would you accomplish this? You would disguise your hatred and pretend to be their Father's friend at first. Once they'd let you into their lives, you'd start subtle whispers that appealed to their egos:

■ *Why did your Father give your sister that gift instead of you?*
■ *Look at your brother. He always has to get all the attention. Your brother likes art, and everyone tells him he's so good at it! I think art is disgusting and offends God, don't you?*
■ *Look at your sister studying science. Everyone knows that your God disagrees with science . . . You should say something about this to your brothers and sisters. She shouldn't be allowed to come around.*

Your lies would start to get more specific as you became entrenched in their lives, because hatred can't really take root without self-loathing.

- *You're so ugly. Look at how your sister looks down on you.*
- *Your brother is smart, and you're stupid. He thinks he's better than you.*
- *You'll feel better if you drink this or snort that.*

And finally: *Why do you go on living? No one likes you anyway. At least if you were dead, they'd appreciate you. They'd feel bad for how they'd treated you.*

God has already defeated Satan! Sometimes we get this idea, probably from other religions, of an equal duel between good and evil happening in the heavens. This is not the case. Satan was defeated and cast out! The only duel now is for your heart and mine. Satan can't touch God, so he attacks His children. And he does this by exploiting the Fall. He does it by appealing to the prideful nature in each of us.

With the Fall, four great separations occurred, according to Genesis 3:

1. **People became hostile to one another.** Adam blamed Eve.
2. **People became hostile to nature.** Nature became cursed and became a source of labor for him.
3. **People became hostile to themselves.** Adam felt shame and hid from God.
4. **People became hostile to God.** When God asked him what had happened, Adam blamed God, saying, "The woman *You* gave me did it."

It's no surprise, then, that Satan exploits these separations. He seeks to push our flesh in its natural direction, toward hatred of one another, nature, ourselves, and God. As James wrote, "If you have bitter envy and selfish ambition in your heart, don't brag and deny the truth. Such wisdom does not come from above but is earthly, unspiritual, demonic" (3:14–15). The Spirit of God unifies and makes peace, while Satan divides. When we create unity among others, even at the expense of our own ambition, when we authentically build others up, and when we serve, we display the Spirit of God. When we gossip, slander, act out of jealousy, and create division, we show that we're following the voice of Satan, acting as enemies of our Savior and Creator.

What does Satan want? He wants to hurt God by separating Him from His children and by separating His children from one another.

How Can We Tell When Satan Is at Work?

The coming of the lawless one is based on Satan's working, with all kinds of false miracles, signs, and wonders, and with every unrighteous deception among those who are perishing. They perish because they did not accept the love of the truth in order to be saved. (2 Thessalonians 2:9–10)

He also performs great signs, even causing fire to come down from heaven to earth in front of people. He deceives those who live on the earth because of the signs that he is permitted to perform on behalf of the beast, telling those who live on the earth to make an image of the beast who had the sword wound and yet lived. (Revelation 13:13–14)

Clearly, Satan can perform miracles and cause people to do so. Many Christians have been led astray by false teachers who have performed great signs. How do we tell the difference?

- When the Spirit of God is at work, all the glory goes to Jesus. When Satan is at work, the glory goes to people.
- The Spirit of God always brings peace. Satan always brings stress and anxiousness.
- The Spirit of God always brings unity and equality. Satan seeks to divide and elevate some people over others.
- The Spirit of God always brings clarity. Satan brings complication and confusion. "How can we really understand what truth is?" ask his servants. It's the same lie he told Eve at the beginning. "Did God really say . . ." (Genesis 3:1). Yes, He did.

What Are We Being Warned About?

When the church is divided, the cause is often false leaders in the church who, out of ignorance, laziness, or greed, tend to complicate the gospel, adding some form of works, tradition, or hierarchy. This allows one group of people to elevate themselves over another, selling out the free gospel of Jesus and controlling others. Jesus is not unaware of their schemes, as we'll see when in a later chapter we study the story of the Judge and His condemnation of the sinful churches. Satan has schemes and tactics to mislead believers and separate us from God's grace and protection. He seeks to entrap Christians:

> I have done this so that we may not be taken advantage of by Satan. For we are not ignorant of his schemes. (2 Corinthians 2:11)

> Put on the full armor of God so that you can stand against the tactics of the Devil. (Ephesians 6:11)

> He must have a good reputation among outsiders, so that he does not fall into disgrace and the Devil's trap. (1 Timothy 3:7)

The final passage is talking about church elders or pastors. So we see that Satan is scheming to entrap people, even pastors. We saw earlier that he disguises himself as an angel of light and uses people to do the same, misleading those who believe in God (see 2 Corinthians 11:13–14). So how can we know the truth when there might be false Christian leaders all around us, some doing miracles? We must be absolutely surrendered to Christ. It is our egos and our flesh that are deceived. When we die to self, the simplicity of the gospel and the peace of God, "which surpasses every thought" (Philippians 4:7), fill us. Take these verses to heart:

I fear that, as the serpent deceived Eve by his cunning, your minds may be seduced from a complete and pure devotion to Christ. (2 Corinthians 11:3)

He will cause deceit to prosper through his cunning and by his influence, and in his own mind he will make himself great. He will destroy many in a time of peace; he will even stand against the Prince of princes. Yet he will be shattered—not by human hands. (Daniel 8:25)

Be serious! Be alert! Your adversary the Devil is prowling around like a roaring lion, looking for anyone he can devour. (1 Peter 5:8)

Who Should Fear Satan?

Believers who are walking in obedience to God's Word have nothing to fear because they are protected by Christ. "He has rescued us from the domain of darkness and transferred us into the kingdom of the Son He loves" (Colossians 1:13). However, when we knowingly commit sin, we open ourselves up to Satan's deception.

We must exercise patience with those who are not walking with Christ, because their minds are blinded. "Perhaps God will grant them repentance leading them to the knowledge of the truth. Then they may come to their senses and escape the Devil's trap, having been captured by him to do his will" (2 Timothy 2:25–26).

To those who have the truth, the arguments of unbelievers are senseless, but we mustn't condemn them or curse them but pray for them. Consider the following verses:

When anyone hears the word about the kingdom and doesn't understand it, the evil one comes and snatches away what was sown in his heart. (Matthew 13:19)

In their case, the god of this age has blinded the minds of the unbelievers so they cannot see the light of the gospel of the glory of Christ, who is the image of God. (2 Corinthians 4:4)

Only prayer and patience will unlock the minds of unbelievers so they can see the truth.

How Do We Fight Him?

As we will see time and again, Scripture calls us to be in a fight. The first call is to fight against Satan. Consider these verses:

Put on the full armor of God so that you can stand against the tactics of the Devil. For our battle is not against flesh and blood, but against the rulers, against the authorities, against the world powers of this darkness, against the spiritual forces of evil in the heavens. This is why you must take up the full armor of God, so that you may be able to resist in the evil day, and having prepared everything, to take your stand. (Ephesians 6:11–13)

I am not praying that You take them out of the world but that You protect them from the evil one. (John 17:15)

Submit to God. But resist the Devil, and he will flee from you. Draw near to God, and He will draw near to you. (James 4:7–8)

Our battle is not against flesh and blood, but against the rulers, against the authorities, against the world powers of this darkness, against the spiritual forces of evil in the heavens. (Ephesians 6:12)

Satan is a liar. His power comes through appealing to our pride and our flesh. If we're surrendered to God, Satan has no hold on us because our lives will be shielded by the armor of God. We want to know who he is and what his schemes are so that we can recognize when he is deceiving us or others. We too often engage the lie rather than the liar.

Life according to the flesh, which is under perpetual harassment by Satan and his lies, always brings pride, discord, and division. Life according to the Spirit always brings humility, peace, and unity. Satan uses the same tactics he did thousands of years ago because they have always worked. He moves among us, appealing to our need to know and to our pride. These are still his main temptations to God's people.

Now we see the immense responsibility that God has given to each of us. We must humble ourselves so that we can fight. Once we know what is wrong with us and who our enemy is, we are ready to become the men God has called us to be. In the next chapter, we'll look at the first step toward becoming servant kings—letting go of any confidence in ourselves to accomplish God's plans on our own. For many of us, this means being completely broken. For some of us, it means weeping bitterly. Let's take a look at Peter and see how Jesus broke a very strong and talented man.

Chapter 4

THE ROCK

If we are truly converted, we shall not only be turned and converted from sinful self, but we shall be converted from righteous self.

> —GEORGE WHITEFIELD, "Repentance and Conversion"

The Lord turned and looked at Peter. So Peter remembered the word of the Lord, how He had said to him, "Before the rooster crows today, you will deny Me three times." And he went outside and wept bitterly.

> —LUKE 22:61–62

he cold moonlight outlined the olive trees like decaying skeletons. Death was in the air. Peter stared down the valley, struggling to keep his eyes open.

He'd had an amazing evening with his Lord and friend, Jesus, but it had also been intensely emotional. James and John were asleep, but Peter fought to stay awake. He looked around the garden and shivered. Jesus was a stone's throw away, sobbing.

Peter adjusted the sword strapped to his leg. He wasn't used to it, and the hilt dug into his side. During dinner, Jesus had said something about selling their cloaks to buy swords because they would soon be considered outlaws (Luke 22:36–37). There were two swords lying in the room where they'd had dinner. Peter had grabbed one and belted it to his waist. They might come to get Jesus, but Peter would fight to the death to defend Him.

Jesus had washed their feet during dinner, imploring them to serve one another. Instead, they'd argued about which of them was the greatest. With His usual patience, Jesus had explained to them again that the greatest was the one who served.

Peter got it, even if the rest of them didn't. He felt superior. It was Peter who always stood for what was right. It was Peter who got out of the boat and walked halfway to Jesus on water while the rest of them cowered. It was Peter who was the first to declare that Jesus was the Messiah—the Son of God. But during dinner, as Peter had tightened the sword around his waist, Jesus turned on him: "You will deny me three times before the rooster crows tomorrow morning, Peter."

It was a punch to the gut. Peter was hurt and shocked. It was as if Jesus didn't know him at all! "I'll die for You, Jesus!" he yelled. He placed his hand on the hilt of the blade. "Even if everyone else runs away," he said, pointing to the others in the room, "I won't!"

Now, lying against the gnarled trunk of an olive tree, Peter watched his breath drifting upward in the cold air. It was unusually chilly for early spring. *Why doesn't Jesus trust me? Why can't He see that I would do anything for Him?* he thought. John's and James's breathing was hypnotic. Peter fought off sleep to keep watch for any enemies, but he was overcome and drifted off.

"Can't you stay awake with Me while I pray?" Jesus's voice awakened Peter and the others. He was standing near them, and His words caused Peter deep shame. *I've let my friend down again.*

Jesus's face looked drawn and pale. His clothes were bathed in sweat. "The time has come," He said.

Even as He spoke, they heard heavy footsteps approaching, along with the murmur of angry voices. Shadows cast by the lanterns of an approaching mob grew more defined. Peter leaped to his feet and drew the sword. The men in the mob passed close enough so the disciples saw they held swords and clubs. Peter also recognized some temple police in the crowd.

Jesus, still standing in the shadows, asked some in the mob, "Who are you looking for?" He already knew the answer.

"Jesus of Nazareth!" they shouted.

"I am He." Jesus knew that His time of torture and death had arrived.

The crowd jumped back from Him and fell down. There was something going on here that they couldn't understand. Their swords and clubs seemed worthless in the face of such humble power.

As they struggled to their feet, Peter, unable to contain himself, lunged forward, swinging his sword at the closest person. It was the clumsy, looping swing of an untrained fisherman, not a skilled soldier. Even so, the slave boy he attacked could not avoid the blow. Peter's sword caught the edge of his ear and severed it, blood spurting from the wound. Peter jumped back, still holding the weapon awkwardly above his head, looking wildly left and then right. "Sheathe your sword!" Jesus commanded him. Jesus picked up the slave boy's ear and placed it back on his head, healing him. The mob, still reeling from the presence of the man they were trying to arrest, hesitated. The disciples saw their opportunity and ran. Peter stood his ground for a moment, but as his rage faded and reason returned, he realized he couldn't protect Jesus. He dropped the sword and hid.

Trailing from a distance, Peter saw the mob take Jesus to the high priest's house. Most in the crowd were stopped in the courtyard, and Peter could get no closer. Some soldiers were warming themselves by a fire, and Peter shouldered his way toward the blaze. He watched Jesus through a lattice while rubbing his hands to keep warm.

Peter tried to fit in with the Romans, talking to them with fake confidence. His charade worked until a slave girl recognized his Galilean accent. "Aren't you one of that man's disciples?" she asked.

Peter hesitated but then heard the thud of a fist striking Jesus. Fear shot through him and he turned on her. "I don't know what you're talking about!" he said. Peter scowled into the fire and looked at the drawn faces of the soldiers. His denial had been too emphatic, and now they looked at him suspiciously. None of them liked it in Judea. The Jews hadn't accepted their fate like the other nations that had been conquered by Rome. There were continuous contention and rioting. The Zealot party was actively killing Roman soldiers who were caught unaware. One of Jesus's disciples had been a Zealot, and the Romans were suspicious of Jesus's followers. The soldiers were cold, tired, and in a bad mood. They were looking for a fight.

One of the soldiers was bigger than the rest. He had a thick chest and broad shoulders. His cold black eyes looked Peter up and down. "You aren't one of His disciples too, are you?" The shadows cast by the fire made his face look like a skull. A few of the other soldiers turned toward Peter, frowning. One of them looked as if he was ready to throw a punch. If he did, the others would follow.

"I am not!" Peter said defensively. He looked around with bravado, then uneasily turned back to the fire. He was no longer welcome in their conversation and was relieved to be left out. He strained to hear the discussion from inside, where Jesus was. There was some yelling, and he caught a glimpse of the high priest tearing his clothes and then screaming "Blasphemy!"

The Romans didn't understand what was happening, but they felt the tension. When the Jews got riled up, bad things happened, and they were really riled up at this Jesus person. The soldiers looked again at Peter to see if he was going to be a problem.

The members of the crowd inside the high priest's house were furious and poured out into the courtyard, pushing Jesus violently in front of them. One of them punched Him, and Jesus struggled to stay on His feet. The soldiers next to Peter stiffened and their muscles clenched. They placed their hands on the hilts of their swords, ready to strike.

It was then that another slave walked over to the fire and recognized Peter. "You're one of them too!" he yelled. "I saw you in the garden!"

The soldiers turned on Peter. Now he was scared and desperate. He'd seen men killed by the Roman soldiers for causing less trouble than this. He cussed and yelled, "I am not one of them! I don't even know the man!"

A rooster crowed. Jesus, blood streaming down His face, looked at Peter with love in His eyes. He stared right into Peter's soul before He was punched again and pushed through the courtyard and out of sight.

Peter ran from the courtyard and wept bitterly.

Confidence in Self

Before this tragic moment, Peter already was a great man of God. He had abandoned everything for Jesus (Matthew 19:27). It was to Peter that God the

Father had revealed Jesus's identity as the Messiah, Son of the living God. It was Peter whom Jesus had blessed and on whom He promised to build His church. It was Peter whom Jesus had renamed the "rock" (Matthew 16:16–18). Peter was a really "good" Christian.

Yet despite sacrifice, faith, and obedience, Peter failed in a tragic way. When his beloved Messiah looked at him amid his denials, this was the last time Peter would see Him before Jesus was tortured to death. Imagine the complete heartache Peter was left to suffer as his beloved friend was killed. As the other disciples mourned the death of their leader, Peter harbored the secret that the last time Jesus saw him, he was denying Him to save himself.

Peter had to be broken of the confidence that he could bring about God's kingdom through his own efforts. Peter had to learn that only God can do the work and that he was but a tool that needed to be yielded to the Father. Before Jesus could truly fill him with the Holy Spirit, Peter had to go outside and weep bitterly. A few months earlier, only moments after Peter had declared Jesus to be the Son of God, Peter even rebuked Jesus at His declaration that He must die (Matthew 16:22).

Peter had the nerve to rebuke the man he had just identified as the Son of God. Back then, Peter—the great man of God—still trusted in himself and in his opinion of spiritual things. He had surrendered his possessions and his identity but not his old self. Still there, competing with the words and even the presence of Jesus, was Peter's idea of how things should be, as opposed to what Jesus said they were. Peter was sure that if Jesus would just tell him what the plan was, he would get it done.

Christ told Peter that he must deny self, that its every claim to its rights must be rejected (Mark 8:35; Luke 9:23). Peter learned a valuable truth in an awful, painful way. There are only two options: we must deny self or we must deny Christ.

After weeping bitterly and even after learning that Jesus had risen from the dead, Peter was left in this state of confusion and guilt. He had to live in the lonely darkness as to where his relationship with Jesus stood until Jesus sought him out (John 21). Jesus made Peter wait until the lesson was fully learned. Then, in a wonderful encounter of grace, Jesus restored Peter and renewed the closeness of their relationship.

A few days later, Peter, now devoid of any confidence that he could accomplish God's will through his own effort, was filled with the Holy Spirit, and his glorious ministry began (Acts 2).

Godliness

Much of the damage done to God's people and the unity of His church has come through people who genuinely love Him but haven't learned to truly trust Him to do the work. We see here three important points:

1. You may be an earnest believer who loves Jesus very much but in whom the self is still very strong. Remember, before Peter denied Jesus, he had cast out demons and healed the sick (Luke 9:1). No matter how high our highs, we are in danger of an awful fall as long as the self reigns in us.

2. Jesus will reveal our unhealthy reliance on self as He continues to use us. Jesus knew who Peter was even as He said that He would build His church on him. Notice that Jesus, even as He was walking from the high priest's house to be tortured, took the time to give Peter a look of love. In the moment of His greatest trial, Jesus still thought of Peter's growth.

3. Just because God is using people doesn't mean that selfishness and an overreliance on self are not still reigning in their lives. It doesn't matter whether they lead a megachurch, perform miracles, or have given away all their possessions to the poor; we must never put our confidence in other believers. The Bible is full of the failures of people who loved God dearly. We must seek to emulate Christ only. As we look to any person as the epitome of godliness, we will be disappointed and risk falling into a pit ourselves.

The most difficult thing to see, as we shift from an entrenched view of self-effort to a life of surrender through daily death to self, is that it is God

Himself who enables us to surrender. God is working in us throughout the entire process of our lives to teach us to yield to Him. Self insists that God needs our help. It distorts the perfect work of God with human effort.

In the heart of every Christian is the hunger to be of maximum benefit to our Lord. This desire comes from the Holy Spirit, deposited in the heart of every believer, which longs for relationship with our Father. Yet our old nature, self, is there to say, "It's okay, God. I'll do it. You just sit back and bless the work." New life has been born in us, but the old, fallen nature is there as well—the nature that insists that the Creator of all things needs us somehow.

Many Christians live joyless lives marked by spiritual failure instead of peace and victory. They know that there is something more, but they can't seem to get ahold of it. So they fake it, living proper lives and following man-made rules, never understanding that true relationship with Christ is something that is promised if they will only come to the end of themselves.

This is the state that Peter had to come to, and it was terribly hard for him because his opinion of himself was high. When Peter went outside to weep bitterly, his fall was great and it was desperate, but God could finally change him into one of His great saints.

Growing in Christ is simply learning to fully surrender to God. There is nothing more for us to do. This means accepting every word He has given us in Scripture. It means understanding that self-will and self-effort are the enemies of our souls. It means that dying to self and self-rights must be evident every moment of our lives. Then Christ can have true possession of us. Then, and only then, will we see the power of the Holy Spirit the way Jesus promised we would.

Surrender is the journey we will take together in this book. We are going to learn the practical lessons of being a man. We are going to discuss how to pray, what faith is, how to discern God's will in our lives, and how to be filled with the Spirit. We are going to learn how to truly love and serve one another. But these things are all results of a solid Christian life, not its cause. If we seek these things in our self-effort and will, we will fail, as we have seen so many others do.

As our foundation, we will continue to learn to fall at the throne of grace until we've discovered how to let Christ do all these things in us. Then we will be ready to be God's servant kings. One of the first signs that we're on the right road is beginning to be able to hear His voice. Let's look at that in the next chapter.

Chapter 5

THE VOICE

The Bible was not given for our information but for our
transformation.

—attributed to Dwight L. Moody

At that moment, the Lord passed by. A great and
mighty wind was tearing at the mountains and was
shattering cliffs before the Lord, but the Lord was not
in the wind. After the wind there was an earthquake,
but the Lord was not in the earthquake. After the
earthquake there was a fire, but the Lord was not in the
fire. And after the fire there was a voice, a soft whisper.

—1 Kings 19:11–12

I had a few partners who claimed to be Christians in the LAPD, but none seemed like very good representatives of Christ. So when a new officer transferred into 77th Division from Valley Vice, seeking me out to say that he was a Christian, I was suspicious. In reality, he was different; you could see it from the peace and joy in his eyes.

Most vice cops are known for being a little crazy. The LAPD actually had a one-year limit on an assignment to any vice division because any more than a year of immersion in the sex trafficking, depravity, and child pornography of vice could permanently mess with a man's mind. My new partner was filled with stories about how Christ had kept him so peaceful and alive as a vice cop, but one I never forgot.

West Valley Vice had received complaints of men being lured into an expensive hotel by a beautiful prostitute. Once the customer got to the hotel room, a huge man with a shotgun would appear from a hiding place and rob him.

My partner had gone undercover to the hotel, met the woman, and followed her upstairs. He had a snub-nosed .38 revolver hidden in the crotch of his jeans and asked her if he could search the suite. When he came to the bathroom, he saw that the shower curtain was drawn. He reached up to draw the curtain back when a deep sense of dread stopped him. A voice in his head told him, *Get out of the room now, as fast as you can.* He mumbled to the prostitute that he had to go down to his car to get the money and ran from the room.

He told his partner that he was freaked out and wanted to arrest her then and there. Both vice cops walked into the hotel suite with their two-inch .38 revolvers and were arresting her when the man they'd heard about suddenly appeared with a sawed-off shotgun. His partner grabbed the woman by the throat and yanked her in front of himself for cover. "Drop the shotgun or I kill her!" he screamed. The man dropped it, and they arrested him.

Any ghetto cop can tell you that once the violence is over, there's a weird camaraderie between cop and convict. It's a strange thing. Often we have friendly conversations with the suspect while he's being booked. While processing the man with the shotgun, my partner asked him where he had been hiding. "The shower," he said.

"Did you see me getting ready to pull that shower curtain back?" my partner asked.

"Yep."

"What would you have done if I'd have pulled it back?"

"Blown your brains out," the man said without emotion.

I looked at my partner after he told the story and asked the first question that came to mind. "What was it that told you not to pull back that curtain?"

He smiled. "It was the Holy Spirit, Ken."

"Well, I've never heard God talk to me like that," I said suspiciously.

"Yes, you have, Ken. You just need to learn how to listen."

Which Voice Are You Listening To?

I was twenty-three years old then. I learned to listen. Now I hear His voice clearly.

A big part of hearing His voice is learning to eliminate the other voices taking up space in your mind. A good test taker knows that in a multiple-choice test, you first eliminate the choices you know aren't true so that you can more clearly see which one might be true. If you want to hear the soft voice of God, shut out all the noise competing for your attention.

When my dog, Ginger, got sick, the vet put her on pain medication that put her into a trance. She lay on the ground, staring blankly while people around her talked. I walked into the pet hospital and watched her for a moment, unresponsive and lifeless. When I asked the vet a question, her head shot up and her ears twitched. Despite the drugs, the noise, and all the other voices, Ginger was attuned to my voice.

We must be attuned to our Father's voice. His soft, sweet voice is drowned out, however, in a sea of competing noise. Sin, self-will, selfish ambition, pride, and the cares of the world choke out His voice. These voices get tangled up in our minds to the point where we can't tell one from the other. We think they're all just our thoughts, but they aren't.

When we eliminate the other voices, we hear Him so clearly that it becomes second nature (Psalm 25:14). You don't have to ask what His will is anymore, because you naturally walk in it. His will becomes your will (Romans 12:2)

Romans 7 and 8

If the Bible has a high point, it is the book of Romans, which is like the great summary of Scripture and what it all means. And if Romans itself has a high point, it's chapters 7 and 8.

Romans 7 describes the state of a sinful person—the utter hopelessness of someone who is trying to earn a spot in heaven by being good enough. This chapter mentions the Holy Spirit only once, but it mentions the law more than twenty times. It uses the words *I, me,* and *my* more than fifty times. It is the story of a person trying to be religious and keep all the rules. Paul, the writer of Romans, summed up the futility of all this at the end of the chapter:

"What a wretched man I am! Who will rescue me from this dying body?" (verse 24).

Then Paul—or any wretched person—comes to the end of himself. He realizes his utter hopelessness and throws himself on God's love and mercy. There he finds God, ready to meet him. He couldn't see God through the blindfold of pride, but now he sees Him, waiting, where He has been since before Paul was born. "I thank God through Jesus Christ our Lord!" Paul said (verse 25), finally realizing the key that unlocks a relationship with God. Now he is ready to move into the next chapter.

Romans 8 starts with these awesome words: "Therefore, no condemnation now exists for those in Christ Jesus." In major contrast to Romans 7, Romans 8 mentions the Holy Spirit fifteen times in the first sixteen verses. Paul is learning to walk in the Spirit, not trusting in himself.

Many Christians think that being saved is enough to have intimacy with God. Not so. The saved person says, "I will do what is good," but doesn't have the power to consistently do good. The flesh is still strong. Old habits die hard.

At the very moment he believed, the saved person was given the Holy Spirit as a seal of his belonging to God. Now he must learn to walk in the Spirit. This is the source of strength and freedom from the yoke of sin.

God has called the church to live in the power of the Spirit, but many Christians are still slaves to the flesh. This is why trusting in another Christian to be a representation of Jesus will always lead to disappointment, betrayal, and despair. No one is the perfect representation of Jesus. The Bible is filled with stories of great and godly people failing miserably. No matter how godly you think people are, no matter how famous they are, how big their church is, or what they've accomplished, they will still fail.

Your enemy wants you to be a prisoner of your own thoughts, and his voice keeps you there. Satan knows what you're thinking and wants to pull you into Romans 7. *Feel bad and try harder!* It's easy for him because you have habits of thinking, which you've spent a lifetime building.

We are continually warned in the Bible that the great danger of the Christian life is in returning to bondage. The entire book of Galatians is about that very subject. The power found through hearing God and walking in His Spirit is to dwell always and only in the present. Our strength must be received each moment from the Holy Spirit.

What Tempts You?

"The mind-set of the flesh is death, but the mind-set of the Spirit is life and peace" (Romans 8:6). The things that tempt you say a lot about you, the state of your relationship with God, and your ability to hear His voice. The appeal of the world and its sin diminishes as we grow in Christ. If you struggle with surface sins of the flesh, such as greed, gossip, slander, lying, lust, sexual perversion, and others (see Galatians 5:19–21), then you are still carnal—you're still living in Romans 7, not in Romans 8. This is why there is so little of God's voice, power, and joy in your life.

We don't surrender our wills; instead, we train our wills to choose God and His ways—to choose life—by dying to our sinful nature daily so that we can hear Him. To clearly hear our Lord's voice, we must first become all-in disciples of Jesus.

Do you wonder why God doesn't speak to you the way you want? Take a look at what tempts you and see whether that gives you a clue as to how far you are from Him. Repent and turn violently from your sin and trust Him to help you resist temptation. You will find that when you've made the decision— really made the decision—to turn from your sin, it isn't nearly as hard as you thought it would be. And God is always with you.

That Beautiful Voice

If you believe you are hearing from God, understand that God's voice will always agree with Scripture (2 Timothy 3:16–17). "My sheep hear My voice, I know them, and they follow Me. I give them eternal life, and they will never perish—ever! No one will snatch them out of My hand" (John 10:27–28). We touched on this topic briefly in "The Liar" chapter, but now let's go deeper and really understand the Spirit's voice. We hear His voice in our spirits and in our hearts, and the sound brings peace and joy—even in conviction or correction.

I recently was with a godly man who made a brief, relatively innocent negative comment about someone. The moment after he uttered the words, he said, "I'm so sorry, Father."

"What was that?" I asked.

"Oh, I just heard the Lord say, *Don't do that, son. Don't say that.*"

The man had heard the sweet correction of the Lord, His voice of rebuke. It's gentle and patient, always working in your heart ultimately to draw you closer to Him. He has no other objective.

By contrast, Satan's voice is harsh and prickly: *Oh, you fool! I can't believe you said that! There you go again! You'll never be better. Maybe if you feel really bad about it and try harder, you won't fail next time!*

The Spirit just says softly, *Don't do that, son. Crawl up in My lap and let's work on this together. Build your brother up; don't tear him down, okay?*

Do you want to hear God speak to you? Repent from all known sin, learn to live in the present, and walk away from a habit you probably didn't know you had—listening to the voice of the liar, the enemy of your soul. Then you will hear the Spirit's voice speaking to you all the time, and you'll realize that He has always been speaking.

Like that pride-filled twenty-three-year-old LA cop, you just couldn't hear Him.

Chapter 6

HURT

Christianity is the only religion whose God bears the
scars of evil.

— Os Guinness

He was pierced because of our transgressions,
crushed because of our iniquities;
punishment for our peace was on Him,
and we are healed by His wounds.
We all went astray like sheep;
we all have turned to our own way;
and the Lord has punished Him
for the iniquity of us all.

— Isaiah 53:5–6

Beware of false prophets who come to you in sheep's
clothing but inwardly are ravaging wolves.

— Matthew 7:15

You now understand your sinful nature and have developed a deep desire to fight Satan and rescue others from his hand. Like Peter, you've died to the idea that God needs you and have begun to hear His sweet, soft voice. But you still lack something. You still don't feel like a servant king. One last thing may be holding you back: you need to learn what it means to live fully in Christ's freedom.

I have found that one of the deepest sources of pain is the bondage placed on people by others in the church. If you have been the victim of this, your freedom will come in forgiving those who have hurt you. If you've been guilty of it, turn from it to the freedom that is in Jesus.

Searching for the Real Jesus

I became a Christian when I was five years old. My father had just retired from the LAPD when he walked into a church and received Christ. I was right behind him. I was all in.

I told everyone about Jesus. When I was six, I chased Ricky Nelson through the airport after my mother told me he was a rock star. When I caught up with Ricky, I told him about Jesus. He graciously stood there for five minutes until I handed him a tract and said we hoped to see him in church.

At age five I was completely filled with the Holy Spirit, and at a very young age I was completely yielded to the Lord. It took about ten years of being in the church and around other Christians to diminish my passion.

I was sent to a Christian school that was a very pleasant place, as long as you didn't see movies, dance, listen to rock music, gamble, drink alcohol, or play cards. Smoking was okay because several of our pastors couldn't kick the habit. Sunday mornings, Sunday nights, and Wednesday nights at our church were competitions to see who could follow the man-made rules the best. For me, the competition was every day because the church controlled the school.

When I was twelve, I was forced to sing in a school musical. At a rehearsal, some kids started to rock the long pew we were sitting in. The teachers weren't sure which boys were doing it, so they beat us all for good measure. When my mother saw my blackened backside from middle leg to lower back, she burst into tears. Pink Floyd's album *The Wall* came out at that time. I'd sneak over to my friend's house to listen to the song "The Happiest Days of Our Lives/Another Brick in the Wall," which is about abusive schoolteachers, because I felt like at least that rock group understood what I was going through. The thing was, even at that young age, I knew the God who lived in me, and He wasn't what the teachers and many other Christians portrayed. Their god had a lot of rules, none of which were in the Bible, and He was really angry. Almost all the students who went to that school fell away from the faith as they grew older. That didn't happen to me though. I poured myself into the Bible. I was just twelve, but I committed to reading three chapters of the Bible every day, searching for the Jesus who I knew was living in my heart. And I found Him—everywhere in the Bible as I read. But search as I could, I couldn't find their Jesus.

By the time I was fifteen, I knew God's Word well. I knew it by choice and I loved it. I began to ask tough questions in class. I was a soft-spoken kid, and it wasn't from rebellion that I asked but from a hungry heart. The things they taught just didn't align with what I was reading in the Bible. The Jesus I read about said that He had come to set us free (John 8:36), but their Jesus seemed to have everyone in a cage. Since the teachers couldn't answer my questions, they thought I was being rebellious and often threw me out of class. I was confused as to what I'd done wrong but relieved that I was too big to beat anymore.

My sophomore year of high school, I had over fifty detentions. They weren't for asking questions but because the teachers didn't like my "attitude." During the spring of that year, I worked hard to earn the money to go on a summer backpacking trip with the church youth group to the Wallowa Mountains in eastern Oregon. Every day after school, on projects arranged by the church, I'd transplant trees at nurseries, cut down huge fir trees and mend fences on ranches, or do construction work. The church credited me $1.50 toward the trip for each hour that I worked.

When summer came, my youth-group leader said I wasn't welcome back at the school or in the youth group. It was like a punch to the gut because he had been the only leader in the church I trusted. The leaders of the church and school had appointed him as their spokesman. He told me I was never to speak to anyone at school or in youth group again.

I asked the youth pastor, "What about the backpacking trip?" He explained that was a no-go, and the church kept the money I'd worked so hard for.

Because my father was asking similar questions about Christ, our entire family was removed from the church. Since my entire life had revolved around the place since I was eight years old, I lost literally every friend I had.

Two Covenants

This wasn't to be the only time I was hurt by false religion; it was just the first time. You've probably been hurt by religion or religious people too. Here's the thing: true Christianity isn't a religion; it's the truth, and its foundation is freedom. The fact that it is a religion to many people shows the failure of God's followers to understand Him and His message.

There are two basic covenants—the old and the new. The old covenant came from the law and was given to Israel. The law is what the godless—who either are confused or are purposely looking to confuse others—like to quote to make the Bible look silly. It is the part of the Bible that talks about not eating pork or how to treat lepers or how to butcher an ox. The point of the law was to show people that it was impossible to keep all its provisions. Through the law God wanted to show people that they couldn't earn their way to heaven. The law allowed God's chosen people—Israel—to be separate from the other nations, but it ultimately compelled those who truly loved Him to cry out, "I can't do this! God, help me!"

When Jesus, who kept the law perfectly, died and rose again, He fulfilled the law for all people (Matthew 5:17), so we are no longer subject to it. Before Christ, the high priest of the Jewish religion would enter the temple's holy of holies (a sacred room), which was behind a thick veil, once a year to offer sacrifices for the people (Hebrews 9:7). When Jesus died on the cross, that veil was miraculously torn in two (Matthew 27:51) to show that all who belong to Christ are now welcomed into the holy of holies. Thus, all who put their faith in Him are priests, completely forgiven (1 Peter 2:9). Through Christ's sacrifice on the cross, the law was fulfilled for each of us. The old covenant had value only in showing people what sin was and their hopelessness to deliver themselves. As long as people are ignorant of this, they have no hope of living in the new covenant. Until they are brought to an intense longing for deliverance from sin and the freedom that brings, they will always fall back into sin and the law (rules).

The sad truth is that many Christians continue to live under the old covenant, striving for God's affection by following rules and living in judgment of those who don't keep them. Sometimes even Scripture is used to abuse people. These judgmental "old covenant" Christians minimize the sins that tempt them while excoriating others for the sins they are struggling with. The result is that many broken people are trapped in guilt that doesn't come from God. They failed at rules made by people, not our heavenly Father.

The apostle Paul, in his first letter to the church in Corinth, presented a list of people who won't "inherit God's kingdom." The list includes homosexuals, the greedy, and verbally abusive people (1 Corinthians 6:9–11). How often do we condemn someone struggling with homosexuality and then turn and say hurtful things to our wives or children? Does this not make us verbally abusive? Or have we condemned someone for yelling at his kids in a restaurant and then left a stingy tip because we were greedy?

Jesus is a lover of the repentant. He has no tolerance for those living in defiant sin, but He has limitless patience for the struggling but repentant. I am not excusing any sins, but I am saying that hurling insults at our children in an unguarded moment breaks our Lord's heart the same as greed or sexual perversion does. Yet He reaches out with grace to those who confess and seek to turn from their sins.

Let's give all repentant people on the sin list in 1 Corinthians the same grace we expect God to give us.

Equality

> There is no Jew or Greek, slave or free, male or female; for you are all
> one in Christ Jesus. (Galatians 3:28)

> Do nothing out of rivalry or conceit, but in humility consider others as
> more important than yourselves. Everyone should look out not only
> for his own interests, but also for the interests of others. (Philippians
> 2:3–4)

As we saw in chapter 4, "The Rock," we seek to elevate self above all—including other people. We use race, gender, intellectualism, social status, occupation, where we live, our college, and anything else to feel superior to others. Racism, sexism, and any other form of discrimination are forms of self-worship, elevating self above others.

Treating all people as equals glorifies God because in doing so, a person turns from the need to worship self and honors God's natural order in creation.

Christ came above others in race as a Jew but served Gentiles. He came beneath others as a working-class man but demanded the respect of the ruling class. He came above others as a man (in ancient society) but served the lowliest of women. He came above all as a perfect man but died for sinners. Jesus is our example. He treated no one as below Him and none as above Him.

This does not mean we don't have roles that require authority. God has given government officials leadership over the governed (Romans 13:1–7; Titus 3:1), husbands over wives (Colossians 3:18; Ephesians 5:22–24; 1 Peter 3:1–6), parents over children (Colossians 3:20; Ephesians 6:1–2), and elders over younger people (1 Peter 5:5).

The CEO of an organization has authority within it and usually makes more money than other employees. Yet he or she is no more valuable in the eyes of God than anyone else. That leader may have more value to the organization because of experience and track record, but not as a person. People who are in love with Jesus Christ treat everyone, especially those under their leadership, as equals.

The Inequality of False Religion

Much of false religion is the application of rules that allow some to elevate self over others. To a person for whom temperance comes easy, religion has a list of don'ts: don't drink, don't smoke, don't dance. Those who find it easy to obey the rules can look down on those who haven't kept them. They can walk by a homeless man in the cold, castigating him for the bottle of wine in his hand, and not offer to help find healing for his soul.

The opposite type of person can be just as godless. Rather than adding rules to God's Word, like the first type of person, these people detract from it. They ignore certain scriptures that don't agree with their worldview and judge others for not seeing God's "freedom."

I was in a large meeting of Christian leaders when a pastor of a large church took issue with some of the harsh words Christ had for some people.

"I don't choose to believe in that Jesus," he said. "The Jesus I believe in was always loving to all people and wouldn't be rude."

"The only Jesus we know is the one presented to us in the Bible," I answered. "If you don't believe in the Jesus of the Bible, then you don't believe in Jesus. You just believe in an idol called Jesus." False religion is simply spiritual pride. Jesus wraps His arms around the person who longs to give up sin, including prejudices and self-will, and to give all to follow Him. Giving away our rights to determine our own path in life is another leap of faith, much like becoming saved. We wonder, *If I give up all, will Jesus really run to me like the father of the prodigal son did and fill me with joy?* Yes, He will. He always does. Keep your eyes focused on Him and leave the world and its false wisdom, including false religion, behind.

The Uniqueness of Christianity

Two things separate Christianity from all other religions. First, Christianity is the only religion that says you can't save yourself. All other religions betray that their origins are from Satan, the great liar, because they all appeal to ego. They all have a formula for saving ourselves. In essence, if we can become good enough by our own efforts to earn a place in heaven, then we can become like God. That was the original lie that Eve fell for. Only Christianity gives us the hard truth that we are slaves to our sinful nature and that only God in His great mercy and love can save us. We literally have nothing we can do to obtain salvation other than to simply receive it (Ephesians 2:8–9).

Christianity has another distinguishing concept. It is the only religion that calls us to lay down our lives for our beliefs (Matthew 16:24–26). We've seen this theme again and again in this book because it is the central theme of Christianity. If you want to know God, if you want true friendship with Him, you must lay down all, including your rights to your own life. This is pure worship of the God who created you. It is giving back to Him the only thing of value you have to give—yourself.

You might say, "Hold on. Remember the Crusades? Remember the Inquisition? People were murdered in the name of Christianity!" Yes, they were. They were murdered by people who stole Christ's name for their own selfish reasons. The Crusades started as an attempt to reclaim the Holy Land and to defend Europe from Muslim invaders, but they turned into murder and looting in many circumstances by people who used the name of Christianity as an excuse for war (2 Corinthians 11:13–15). They were people still living in slavery to the old covenant instead of living in the freedom of the new.

I once got a call from a close friend who had run into a man I knew. This man had slandered someone else during a meeting, and seeing that my friend was unconvinced, the man said, "Even Ken Harrison knows this is true." Did I know it to be true? No. The acquaintance had stolen my name to give himself credibility. Though he'd used my name, he did not represent me. In fact, he represented the opposite of what I believed.

This has been done to our beloved Savior time and again. Satan uses people who are driven by their ego and self-righteousness to do severe damage to others in the name of Christ. Anyone who uses the name of Christ to control, to hate, to do violence against the innocent, to discriminate, to separate, or to slander is a liar and a thief because that person is usurping the name of Jesus. This is what it truly means to use the Lord's name in vain.

The Equality of Christianity

All God's children are equal in His eyes and equally loved, though we have different gifts and callings. In one of his sermons given in his *Thru the Bible* series, J. Vernon McGee told the story of a megachurch pastor who died and went to heaven. He was getting brought to his mansion by Jesus when they pulled up to a huge, beautiful place. *Wow*, thought the pastor, *this is certainly the place I deserve after building such a huge church.*

"Oh no," said Jesus, "this isn't yours. It belongs to the old widow Mrs. Mahony."

"Who was that?" the pastor asked. They drove out to the suburbs and pulled up to a little cottage. "There must be some mistake, Jesus!" the pastor said. "How could that old widow have such a grand place and me this little cottage? Remember how big a church I built?"

Jesus smiled patiently at him. "Your church was big because Mrs. Mahony spent so much time on her knees praying for it. You had nothing to do with it."

Jesus is no respecter of persons and shows no favoritism (Acts 10:34–35). We may have different roles on earth, and the gifts He gave to some may elevate them in the eyes of society, but those who have given their lives to Him are all equally His children. He will reward His children for what they've done. Those who give little will receive little, and those, like Mrs. Mahony, who pour themselves out for their brothers and sisters in Christ, will receive much (2 Corinthians 9:6).

You may have been wounded by Christians who are living in the old covenant. Forgive them and move on. Don't let bitterness remove you from fellowship with God. Your Father is training you to be a king, and kings don't hold on to hurt. Those old-covenant Christians don't represent Him any more than the man who slandered others and used my name represented me.

Our Father has His hands out to you to come work beside Him, to bring other wounded souls into His joy. When you're done, crawl into His lap. All you can give Him is you.

Chapter 7

HOLINESS

You contribute nothing to your salvation except the sin
that made it necessary.

—attributed to Jonathan Edwards

As the One who called you is holy, you also are to be holy
in all your conduct; for it is written, Be holy, because I
am holy.

And if you address as Father the One who judges
impartially based on each one's work, you are to conduct
yourselves in fear during the time of your temporary
residence.

—1 Peter 1:15–17

This is how we are sure that we have come to know Him:
by keeping His commands. The one who says, "I have
come to know Him," yet doesn't keep His commands, is
a liar, and the truth is not in him.

—1 John 2:3–4

A holy person is different from the crowd; this person is focused on God's will and His Word. A servant king is a holy man, set apart. His identity comes from being a child of God. He may be known for other things—he may be known as a CPA or a Green Bay Packers fan or an expert fisherman—but his overriding identity is a holy man. He is set apart from this world, and that dictates what he does, says, and thinks.

In the LAPD, I wanted to be a gunfighter. I wanted to be a cold-blooded ghetto cop who stood for the kind of justice that exacts vengeance on the wicked first and observes the law second. I thought that's who I was until reality intervened and sent me on one of the most horrific calls of my life.

I was working with Craig, one of my best friends, who was a committed bodybuilder. A sergeant approached us just out of roll call: "Hey, fellas, we got a bad child-abuse situation. I thought you'd be good to handle it."

I stared at the sergeant, and Craig stared at me. There were two calls that no ghetto cop wanted—rape and child abuse—both for the same reasons: they took hours to handle, they were often horrific, and untangling the truth of the situation was difficult. Craig stared at me because he knew why we were picked. I was known as the Christian around the station. Who else but the Christian should go coddle a damaged child?

The sergeant gave me a shrug and a "What can I do?" look. Craig looked at me like he wanted to kill me. He didn't say a word as we drove to the day care to meet a little girl I will remember until the day I die.

I wasn't married and had no kids. We arrived and I looked at the five-year-old girl across from me. She was beautiful and smiling, and I had no idea how to talk to her. I still remember her yellow dress and the matching ribbon in her hair. I remember her teacher saying that the girl screamed when she urinated. I also still remember the little girl's innocent face as she described sexual intercourse to me in detail. That was what had happened to her every week with her father, her uncle, and her father's best friend.

Have you ever seen evil reflected in the eyes of an innocent victim—a victim too innocent to have figured out how to shroud the offense in bitterness? As she played with a pencil, the girl described to us the evil she'd gone through with no hatred or shame, just sadness.

We took her to the hospital for medical treatment and then to her mother. The mother had left the father a few months earlier, and that would normally have been the end of it for us. Once we established the little girl was safe with her mother, we would leave and refer the case to the child-abuse detectives, except for what the mother said as we were leaving: "I'm worried about my son. He's with their father."

We froze. Her two-year-old son was with the father. We needed to get him. Now.

The father lived only two miles away, and we drove quickly to his apartment. If I'd been older and wiser at that time, it would have saved a lot of heartache. It also would have saved my index finger. I wasn't old enough to understand that if I had a five-year-old daughter, I'd respond to things differently. I didn't have a daughter, but my partner, Craig, did—a beautiful five-year-old—and she looked a lot like the girl we'd just left.

We climbed the filthy stairs of an old apartment to meet a man who was a monster. He'd broken the most sacred trust in the world. He was a father who had stolen the innocence of his own daughter. I stood in the dark just outside a dilapidated door, drew my pistol, and kicked the door off its hinges.

The father jumped out of bed. He was naked, and so was the toddler who was in bed with him. I holstered my gun and crossed the room, closing my left fist around the man's throat and starting to throw a punch with my right. Craig's massive forearm swept me back from the man as he jammed his Beretta 9mm against the man's head and started to pull the trigger.

From the corner of my eye, I could see the boy standing on the bed, staring at us. I jammed my finger behind the trigger on Craig's weapon just as he pulled it. With my finger behind the trigger, he couldn't pull it far enough to fire the 9mm. Craig screamed and cussed as we fell to the ground and fought for at least thirty seconds. I kept punching him with my free hand as he twisted the gun, trying to free it. I fought as if my life depended on it, because it very well might have. If he'd freed his gun and murdered that man, he might not have left witnesses.

At that moment a lieutenant appeared in the door, shocked to see his officers on the ground, fighting over a gun. It was strange to see him there because lieutenants normally didn't leave the station. Craig's shock at seeing our commanding officer standing over us was enough for me to get his gun away from him and slide it to the lieutenant.

We booked the father and got the boy safely to his mother. The lieutenant never did say anything about it. We finished our reports as the sun was rising near the end of our shift, omitting the part about nearly executing a man. Craig looked at me with disgust. "You should have let me kill him," he said. "He'll just hurt more kids." Craig asked for a new partner the next day, and he never talked to me again.

Nature

Our true nature, who we really are, is revealed in the unexpected moments. In the moments when we don't have a chance to think about what we should do, that's when we see who we really are. How do you react when you are insulted, get cut off on the freeway, or don't get the credit you think you deserve? What is your reaction when a situation arises and you've had no time to prepare yourself?

When the sun rose on the day we met that five-year-old girl, I would have been sure I'd have killed the man in that situation. That's because I believed I was a ruthless cop ready to dole out violent justice. Instead, I fought to save his life. Why? In a moment of panic and stress, my nature was revealed. I wasn't the gunfighter that I wanted to believe I was. I was a Christian, a follower of Jesus. Without time to prepare my thoughts and actions to align with what I wanted to believe of myself, thankfully my true nature emerged.

If I asked you to complete the sentence "God is _____," what would you say? If you said "love," you'd be right, but only in part. That answer misses the fullness of His nature. Both in the New Testament and the Old, God declared that His nature is holiness.

When Isaiah was in heaven, the angels around God called out, "Holy, holy, holy is the LORD of Hosts" (Isaiah 6:3). They shouted out His nature to one another. In Revelation 4:8, we see that it will always be this way. In that verse, which is describing the future, the creatures never cease saying "Holy, holy, holy" in God's presence.

The Bible from beginning to end documents God's nature as *holy*. God's holiness is what makes the reality that He died for our sins and loves us so utterly amazing. If you don't understand God's holiness, you can't understand the extent of His love.

If you heard that a man named John forgave his friend a debt, you might think John's a nice guy. If you heard that John forgave his friend a debt of a million dollars, you'd have a completely different understanding of how nice John is.

The distance between God's holiness and our sin is so large that it's like our sin is an infinite debt. This is why teaching about God's love and forgiveness is really incomplete without a true understanding of His holiness. When we understand His holiness, we understand the limitlessness of His love, and then we yearn to be what He wants us to be. And what does God expect our nature to be? "Be holy, because I am holy" (1 Peter 1:16).

So how do we become more holy? By now you should know the answer: by dying to our rights to ourselves. This causes God's nature increasingly to become our nature. The beginning of this is self-control. Let's take a look at this.

Holy Nature

The fruit of the Spirit is love, joy, peace, patience, kindness, goodness, faith, gentleness, self-control. (Galatians 5:22–23)

Make every effort to supplement your faith with goodness, goodness with knowledge, knowledge with self-control, self-control with endurance, endurance with godliness, godliness with brotherly affection, and brotherly affection with love. For if these qualities are yours and are increasing, they will keep you from being useless or unfruitful in the knowledge of our Lord Jesus Christ. (2 Peter 1:5–8)

How can you know if you're a righteous man? Can you trust your own opinion of yourself? Hitler, Stalin, and Mao probably didn't look in the mirror and say, "Wow, I am a villain!" In fact, they were impressed with themselves, despite having slaughtered many people. To have risen to such heights, they probably were smarter and much more gifted than we are, so if they can be so deceived about their own state, so can we. Because of the fall of humanity, we naturally tend toward worshipping ourselves, and we have an enemy who is always pushing us in that direction. So how can we know?

The scriptures quoted above contain two lists that describe a godly or holy person. We must learn what God says a godly person looks like, not trust our own faulty opinions. Notice that the fruit of the Spirit is a list of characteristics, given to us by Paul, that are the result of something—crucifying the flesh and living by the Spirit (Romans 8:13). Do the qualities of love, joy, peace, patience, kindness, goodness, faith, gentleness, and self-control typify your life?

If not, let's look at the second passage. Here Peter gave us a different list of the characteristics of a godly person. Notice, though, that his list is not the results of a life lived in the Spirit but is a list of things we are to "make every effort" to do. Peter assumed we have faith, which is the starting point of salvation; then he exhorted us to add goodness, knowledge, self-control, endurance, godliness, brotherly affection, and love. In essence, making every effort to do the things on Peter's list will make us people who naturally demonstrate the things on Paul's list.

Only two of the characteristics appear in both passages: self-control and love. Paul listed the characteristics of a Spirit-led life, starting with the most important quality: love. Peter gave a list that builds on itself, each quality leading to the next, which ultimately results in the most important one: love. Thus, we can't have true love unless we have self-control.

This book intends to show the path toward being real men, which will allow us to live on earth in joy and victory and to have a rich welcome into the kingdom of heaven. Here we see the first aspect of such a man: *self-control*.

A friend of mine, Steve Brown, is a well-known pastor and author. He tells the story of a young man coming up to him after a sermon and saying, "I'd love to be all those things you talked about, but I can't."

"Why not?" asked Steve.

"Because I'm a heroin addict," he said.

"Do you want to stop being a heroin addict?" Steve asked.

"Of course!" came the reply.

"Then stop doing heroin," said Steve.

If you knew Steve, this story would be surprising, because Steve is not a brusque, hard person—in fact, he's a gracious and loving man. But in this instance the Lord moved Steve to say what he needed to say to this young man.

A month later, the man returned and let Steve know that he'd given his life to Christ and had stopped doing heroin that same night. "No one ever told me it was that easy," he told Steve.

One of the most important aspects of masculinity is accountability. And the beginning of accountability is self-control. A man takes responsibility. He understands that he and only he is accountable for what is in his charge.

An accountable man seeks to serve in some capacity in all his relationships because he understands that he is responsible for the health of any group of which he's a part, whether it is his family, his church, his work, or any other organization to which he belongs. A passive man looks to take from his relationships. He looks to be served rather than to serve.

One of the ways to destroy society is to destroy masculinity. The way to do this is to have males who are not accountable. How does this happen? Eliminate self-control. If you drink too much, look at pornography, look at things that lead to pornography, are addicted to mood-enhancing drugs, are obsessed with sports, are a workaholic, or _____, you need to stop. Stop now. Your flesh has control of you.

How do you do this? You must walk in the Spirit of God. He will give you the self-control that leads to holiness.

Our Walk

As Andrew Murray wrote in *The Indwelling Spirit,* "Most earnest efforts to abide in Christ, to walk like Christ, fail when we depend more on the wisdom of this world than on the power of God."[7] The greatest hindrance to many Christians becoming truly holy is their trust in their orthodoxy—the sufficiency of their religious knowledge. They are not open to the teaching of the Spirit because they read the Bible with closed minds. Their minds are closed to anything that doesn't agree with what they think they know because their religion says so. What hinders God most is the will and wisdom of this world, and religion and religious philosophies are high on this list. Jesus spent much of His time debating with people who were puffed up in their religious knowledge—so puffed up that they couldn't see God when He was standing right in front of them.

Acting in faith is vitally important because Satan is there, even as we read

God's Word and pray, telling us that knowing is what we're about, rather than doing (James 1:22). Obviously, Bible study is important, but its end is for us to know God and His will for us. He wants us to get in the fight to bring the hurting and lost people around us into fellowship with Him, and we can't do that if we can't even control ourselves.

The first move is on us, to put to death the deeds of the body so that God's Spirit can lead us into a special relationship—a sonship—with Him (Colossians 3:5). Then the attraction to sin will fade, and we will begin to see things through God's eyes—as they really are.

As we see things in this light, we no longer strive to win an impossible battle (Romans 7). Rather, our lives become ones of peace, joy, fulfillment, and blessing to others. Holiness, being set apart to God, becomes our nature, and with it comes self-control. It becomes our identity. The things of this world fade, and our relationship with Jesus Christ becomes our overwhelming desire. It becomes who we are.

Being a gunfighter, being wealthy, belonging to the right club, or being promoted to the highest level of society becomes nothing in comparison with knowing our Lord and obeying His Word. We are on the road to becoming holy.

We have started to become servant kings.

Chapter 8

HUMILITY

It was pride that turned angels into devils. It is humility that makes men as angels.

—AUGUSTINE

Make your own attitude that of Christ Jesus,
who, existing in the form of God,
did not consider equality with God
as something to be used for His own advantage.
Instead He emptied Himself
by assuming the form of a slave,
taking on the likeness of men.
And when He had come as a man
in His external form,
He humbled Himself by becoming obedient
to the point of death—
even to death on a cross.
For this reason God highly exalted Him.

—PHILIPPIANS 2:5–9

Humility is the primary characteristic of a person who is in love with Jesus Christ. No matter what his accomplishments are, he does not have Jesus as the primary love of his life unless humility is the foundation of who he is. It is very hard for men to become truly humble. Many men, including myself, have to be really broken before true humility takes root and our Lord can use them.

When the Lord broke me, it wasn't in a way I could ever have seen coming. A new officer named Don transferred into 77th Division, and we were about to become the perfect partners. He had just finished two years of being undercover with the Hells Angels and Mongols biker gangs in Los Angeles. Don was six foot one and 240 pounds of sheer muscle, and he was completely devoid of fear.

Our division was only eight square miles, but in our little slice of paradise, we were on pace to have over 170 murders that year, largely because of the gang war between the Crips, the Bloods, and 18th Street, a well-funded Mexican gang that was infringing on the traditionally black neighborhoods.

Night after night as we hit the streets, we'd see crime-scene tape with dead bodies from drive-by shootings. Mothers stood outside the tape, sobbing for lost sons. As we ended our shift, we often saw women on their knees, scrubbing blood from the sidewalk in front of their houses. Don and I had seen enough, and we declared war on the gangs. We were assigned to an X car, which was sort of like being a free agent; we didn't have to answer radio calls but could just roam around looking for crime.

Most gangs controlled a very small area, maybe two blocks. They couldn't go outside that area or they risked being killed by the gangs that controlled adjoining blocks. The gangs would stand in their blocks, often in groups of forty to eighty, dealing drugs. They divided the duties of who carried the guns, who carried the drugs, and who carried the money. To be caught with all three was a serious crime; dividing them up was less risky and a lesser crime if caught. We cared only about the guns because usually the gangs entrusted their most murderous members with them.

We perfected the art of identifying which gangsters were carrying guns. The trick was to see them before they saw us. Inevitably, upon seeing the police, someone carrying a weapon would make a barely discernible move with his hand to his waistband to make sure the gun was covered. As we turned the corner onto a heavily gang-infested street, we tried to keep our eyes on the entire group, looking for the ones who made that slight move.

As we got close, the gang members expected us to do the usual, which was to line up ten guys or so and search them. Those with guns and drugs would just slip toward the back of the group, and those with nothing would move into place to get searched. Instead, just as we got close to the gangster we knew was carrying, I'd launch from the car. He'd take off, and I'd chase him from yard to yard and over a few fences. Because of the small area in which he could run and because Don was trolling the street with the car, we'd always catch him.

After any violent arrest like this, the officers had to fill out a use-of-force report. It didn't mean that someone got hurt, only that he didn't come along peacefully.

Don and I set the record for gun arrests by a patrol car two months in a row, averaging over one gun arrest per day. We attracted the attention of the 77th homicide detectives, who started dispatching us to look for murderers they were trying to catch.

Two things happened during this time. The first was that violent crime in the areas we were working dropped dramatically because we were taking away the ability of gang members to rob and murder. The second was that Don and I were racking up use-of-force reports because just about every arrest was a foot pursuit and a fight. Many of the gangsters we caught had arrest warrants for murder, robbery, and rape, and we received numerous commendations for our work.

Don and I became known around the station. Every day we'd show up with a felon and some kind of gun that we'd taken from him shoved in our belts. Normally this would have been a great career builder. Except something happened: *Rodney King.*

The Rodney King incident occurred far north of us in a low-crime, mostly white area we called the Valley. The fallout, however, would be in the high-crime area where we were. Political pressure came from all directions. The federal government started an investigation, and suddenly we had reporters everywhere we went.

Don and I were identified as two of the most aggressive officers in the LAPD. Around the station we were heroes. I was puffed up with pride, but I was about to have my life completely altered.

My uncle had just retired from his position as a captain with the LAPD. He called me down to his house near the beach in San Clemente. I knew exactly where to find him. He spent his mornings sitting on his porch, listening to Rush Limbaugh on his Walkman, and his afternoons fishing for corvina and watching his sons surf.

"So you're a big deal up at 77th, I hear," he said.

I grinned proudly. "Yep."

"You're a fool," he said. I was shocked. "Do you think they identified guys like you because they like you? The politicians are taking control of this department. The LAPD as you and I know it is over. They're identifying the cops who put bad guys in jail so they know whose careers to destroy. You're now top on their list."

"But why?" I was confused. "Every one of our arrests was great. We got commendations. We took awful people off the streets. Crime is dropping like a rock. We have people from the neighborhoods running up to thank Don and me everywhere we go because they're so grateful that someone's actually doing something."

"You're too old to be so naive, Ken," he said. "You're protecting the poor. Politicians don't care about the poor. They care about their careers, and the poor don't help their careers. After this Rodney King thing, they want officers now who will do nothing. Guys like you create problems; you cause lawsuits; you get in shootings—you create bad press for the politicians. They want officers who will do nothing until this all blows over, and that could be ten years from now.

"You're too smart to get stuck in this mess, Ken. Take your wife and move back to Portland by her family and go run a company or something."

So I did. With no plan or job, we moved back to Portland, where we'd both been raised. The country was in a recession, and though the LAPD was a big deal in law enforcement, it didn't mean much in the professional world. I had no idea what to do.

I worked hard at several jobs but didn't really know how to start a new career. I needed to spend time in prayer, seeking God for His wisdom, but I was too proud. I was determined to make myself into something on my own. Besides, I had a fallback—I could always go back to police work. I knew that God wasn't calling me to that and that He had something much better in mind, but I was getting tired of waiting for Him.

Finally I applied to be a police officer in one of the larger Portland suburbs. I didn't want to be a suburban police officer but didn't know what else to do. They were delighted to have someone with LAPD training and experience apply and pushed me to the top of the list. The chief of police assured me that the interviews were only a formality; they were anxious to get me onto the streets as soon as possible.

He was as good as his word. I flew through the process and ignored God all along the way. I had my own plan, and with the LAPD on my résumé, I didn't really need Him.

Just before I was hired, there was one last thing—it was just a formality. The last step was that I needed to appear before some of the citizens of the city to be interviewed. The interview went fine until a woman asked how many felony arrests I'd made. I thought about it briefly and said, "About forty or so."

She looked uncomfortable with the answer, which I didn't understand. The chief intervened. "Officer Harrison, I'm not sure you understood what she was asking. We had another officer in here just before you. He said that he'd made ten felony arrests in ten years. Are you saying that you made forty felony arrests in only three years on the LAPD?"

"No," I said. They looked relieved until I spoke again. "I made forty per month." There were gasps, and the chief looked mortified. And then I said the stupidest thing possible in the moment. "It was the Watts area of LA—you know, Compton. What did you think?"

I got a letter a few days later thanking me for applying but saying that I was overqualified. Now I really was at the bottom. Not long before, I was a well-known officer in the best police department in the world. Now I was being rejected by a small suburban department. Worse, I was being rejected for being good at my job. I had been ready to shortcut God, taking a job that I knew wasn't His plan for me. Now the backup plan I'd been holding on to was off the table.

Finally I was driven to my knees. God had a great plan, but I couldn't be blessed by it while I held on to my own self-sufficiency. Now that my plans were exhausted and there was nowhere to turn, all confidence in self apart from God had been taken away. I finally turned to the Lord, who had been waiting there all along with open arms. In my pride I couldn't see Him.

As I was reading the Bible one night, I came across this promise from

James 1:5: "If any of you lacks wisdom, he should ask God, who gives to all generously and without criticizing, and it will be given to him." I claimed that promise. I asked for forgiveness, for running along in my own understanding. I told God that I was a fool and didn't understand business. I had a wife and soon a family to support and didn't have a clue how I would do it. He promises wisdom to those who ask. I was asking and believed He would keep His promise. And why wouldn't He? He loves each of us, and He was letting me learn the hard way to come to Him when I was in need. He asks us to be like little children, and that's what I became.

After that, I suddenly had very astute business sense. Soon I got a job as a trainee in a commercial real estate firm for $1,050 per month, a third of what I'd been making as a police officer. I was thrilled to get it. Everything came incredibly easy. God had given me wisdom for business instantly, but it had taken me coming to a point of complete dependence on Him. I climbed the ladder quickly. Within five years, I was a partner in the biggest independent firm of its kind in the US.

What Exactly Is Humility?

Humility is clear eyesight. It is the ability to see things as they really are. A servant king is a humble man. A servant king places the needs of those in his care above his own. A servant king doesn't get his identity from what he has accomplished. He gets it from God.

Our flesh and our old nature see through a lens of self. We perceive things based on how they affect us. Pride distorts how we see the world. It causes our identity to be based on our accomplishments or lack thereof.

The thicker our lens of self—our pride—the less we see things as God sees them, which is how they really are. This is evident in the musings of a crazy person. As G. K. Chesterton described in *Orthodoxy,* a madman looks at himself as the center of all things. If he were to recognize that no one actually is focused on him, he would be infinitely happier because his world would suddenly become infinitely bigger.[8]

Pride shrinks the universe to a tiny world in which we are the god. As we die to self, we are able to see the world more clearly, as larger and more wonderful than we can comprehend. Pride is a miserable state because we don't really inflate ourselves or our value. Instead, we shrink the universe to meet our limited imaginations.

One story tells of an old man who stood at the bank of a river, desperately seeking a way to cross. It was bitterly cold, and darkness was closing in. Suddenly he heard the thunder of horses running up behind him. The freezing man jumped to the side of the trail and searched the faces of the riders.

Man after man raced past him, barely noticing him as they plowed across the river. When the last rider approached, the old man stepped into his path and looked long and hard at him. "Sir, would you mind giving an old man a ride to the other side?" he asked.

The rider dismounted and helped the old man into the saddle. Then he remounted his horse and took the old man across the river and all the way to his destination, a small cottage a few miles away.

As they rode into the yard and the rider helped the man down, he asked a question that had been gnawing at him during their cold ride: "Sir," he gently asked the old man, "I notice that you let several other riders pass by without making an effort to secure a ride. Then I come up and you immediately asked me for a ride. I'm curious why, on such a bitter winter night, you would wait and ask the last rider. What if I had refused and left you there?"

"I've been around these here parts for some time," the old man answered. "I reckon I know people pretty good. I looked into the eyes of the other riders and immediately saw there was no concern for my situation. It would have been useless even to ask them for a ride. But when I looked into your eyes, kindness and compassion were evident. I knew, then and there, that your gentle spirit would welcome the opportunity to give me assistance in my time of need."

The rider thanked him for his sentiments and added, "May I never get too busy in my own affairs that I fail to respond to the needs of others with kindness and compassion." With that, President Thomas Jefferson mounted his horse and rode into the night.[9]

Because we are fallen and therefore see things through our pride, we have difficulty judging ourselves properly. The more wicked people are, the higher their opinion of themselves tends to be. In order to properly judge ourselves, we must look at things from outside our own perspective. The way we react to things tells us where we are in our walk with Christ.

The insignificant things of daily life are the things that show us who we are. They show what spirit possesses us. It is our most unguarded moments that show us whether we walk in the Spirit or in the flesh. How do you react when you're tired, hungry, cold, irritated, or stressed? Here we see what Jesus meant when He said, "Whoever is faithful in very little is also faithful in much, and whoever is unrighteous in very little is also unrighteous in much" (Luke 16:10).

People often mistake confidence for pride. Actually, the most confident people are usually the humblest, such as the great saints Abraham, David, Joseph, Paul, and Apollos. The Bible calls Moses, who led an entire nation out of slavery, the humblest man on earth (Numbers 12:3).

Let's look at some aspects of a humble man. Search your heart. Do these characteristics look like you?

- He no longer compares himself with others.
- He seeks no recognition for himself.
- He sees every person equally as a child of God and honors him or her as such.
- He enjoys hearing others praised, even if he is forgotten.
- He forgives.
- His life is marked by patience.
- His relationships are known for peace and unity.
- He encourages others.

We see humility as a virtue, but it is really the symptom of something else—the Holy Spirit reigning in a person as self has become less. The holiest is always the humblest.

Pride doesn't always show up as arrogance. It can appear as self-loathing, shyness, obsession with guilt, or anger. This is because pride always comes from a focus on self.

I once confronted a Christian who was living in sin, and he yelled at me, "Don't you think I feel bad about it?" I asked him what his feelings had to do with anything. Pride thinks that feeling guilty is some sort of penance. Guilt without repentance disregards those whom your sin has hurt. It is just a continued focus on self, simply flipping from arrogance to self-loathing. It's all self.

Humility grows as our Lord is revealed to us. As we come to know the Savior and look up into His face, we become more aware of our own depravity. Not in a self-deprecating way, but with the gratitude of a child who realizes that he is completely dependent on God and that God loves him and has promised to never leave or forsake him (Deuteronomy 31:6; Hebrews 13:5).

Faith and Prayer

You can have deep intellectual conviction about God and strong biblical knowledge, but you can't have effective faith or a strong prayer life when there is pride in your heart. God is moved to answer the prayers of a child who cries out in dependence on Him. As long as we live for the honor and admiration of people and seek security in this world, we will not have effective prayer lives.

Pride makes faith impossible because it keeps confidence in self apart from God. The nearer we are to true humility, the closer God is to fulfilling our every desire. This is because true humility aligns our hearts' desires with God's (Philippians 2:12–13).

Being Exalted

"Humble yourselves, therefore, under the mighty hand of God, so that He may exalt you at the proper time, casting all your care on Him, because He cares about you" (1 Peter 5:6–7). Our job is to humble ourselves. If we do so, we can have faith that God will exalt us. This is simple logic because humility means that we have an audience of One. As humility reaches maturity, our Lord is the only one whose opinion matters, and we seek it each moment. This is not to earn more of His love—that is impossible. It is because our love grows more and more, and we adore the growing closeness of fellowship with Him, which comes as self dies.

> If anyone comes to Me and does not hate his own father and mother, wife and children, brothers and sisters—yes, and even his own life—he cannot be My disciple. Whoever does not bear his own cross and come after Me cannot be My disciple. (Luke 14:26–27)

Courage and Generosity

Humility is the very nature of a servant king and is the foundation of Christianity; everything else is simply a symptom of it. However, there are many people who fake humility. We saw in the chapter entitled "Hurt" that so many people have been wounded by religion, even Christianity. Often this hurt comes from the children of Satan masquerading as children of Christ. So how can we discern who is really humble, those who are really His? There are two distinct outward signs of a humble person: courage and generosity. Let's look at them next.

Chapter 9

COURAGE

The paradox of courage is that a man must be a little careless of his life even in order to keep it.

—G. K. CHESTERTON, *All Things Considered*

Learn to do what is good.

Seek justice.

Correct the oppressor.

Defend the rights of the fatherless.

Plead the widow's cause. . . .

If you are willing and obedient,

you will eat the good things of the land.

But if you refuse and rebel,

you will be devoured by the sword.

—ISAIAH 1:17, 19–20

The Los Angeles Police Department is known as the best police department in the world. It once was the only major police department in the US that did not answer to its city's mayor, making corruption almost nonexistent.

The department has trained special-forces units in several armies, not just for the US military but for units from other countries as well. Historically, Los Angeles was the only major city the Mafia failed to become established in because the LAPD brutally stamped it out when the department was reformed by Chief William Parker in 1950.

The LAPD takes great pride in its reputation, and trust isn't earned easily by new police officers. When we graduated from the academy, we were called "boots," a term that meant we were unproven. We were treated as equals in public, but in the car or at the station, we were treated like children. We had to call fellow officers sir or ma'am and were required to run errands and complete demeaning tasks. This went on for a year or until we proved ourselves in a violent situation.

When I graduated from the academy in 1989, Los Angeles was at the height of the gang wars. The gangs were far better armed than we were. We had to trust in better training and in our fellow officers. For those who worked in the high-crime areas of the city, like Rampart, Newton, Southeast, or 77th Division, it didn't take long for an opportunity to come along to shed the awful "boot" moniker.

Jarius was my academy classmate, my roommate, and one of my best friends. When he was just eleven days out of the academy, Jaruis's time to prove himself came. Hollywood homicide detectives appeared in roll call with a picture of a suspect they were looking for. The man had just killed a police officer in Santa Ana, and they thought he'd come north to LA. Jarius took a copy of the picture and looked down every alley that morning for his boogeyman. The crazy thing was, with 14.5 million people in the metro area of Los Angeles, Jarius found him.

In an alley, Jarius saw a man fidgeting with the open trunk of his car. "Stop the car, sir," Jarius said to his partner. "I think I see the suspect." He pointed to the picture. His partner rolled his eyes and stopped, putting the car in reverse and pulling into the alley. His partner knew you had to patronize the young kids just out of the academy. You didn't just see a cop killer in a Hollywood alley in the middle of the afternoon. Then they found out what the man was fidgeting with in his trunk. He lifted a .30 carbine and filled their car with bullets.

The suspect fled in his car, leading them in a pursuit through afternoon traffic on Sunset Boulevard. With their siren blaring, they chased him at a speed of about twenty miles per hour. Somehow, while driving not much faster than a man can run, the suspect managed to wreck his car pulling into an Arby's.

Jarius was the first one out of the car, and the man opened up on him. Jarius dove behind a newspaper stand and heard the bullets thumping into the newspapers stacked between his head and the shooter. When other police cars streamed into the parking lot, distracting the suspect, Jarius stood up from behind the newspaper stand and shot him in the chest. The muzzle of the carbine tilted upward, and the officers ran toward him, firing. The man died with more than twenty bullets in his chest and head. A young "boot," who would never have to call anyone "sir" again, stood over him.

Not far away from where Jarius passed his test, another young officer named Prescott faced his own. He was one of our academy classmates and the biggest of us all. Built like an NFL linebacker, he looked like the ultimate cop. Prescott went to Hollenbeck Division, better known as East LA, a major Mexican immigrant area of the city.

Prescott was lucky enough to draw a high-crime area and get morning watch, which was from 10:00 p.m. to 6:45 a.m. This was the perfect chance to gain respect quickly. When he and his partner got a call about a burglary in progress, Prescott pulled out his Ithaca shotgun and racked a round into the chamber. His partner, knowing after years on the job that burglary suspects are rarely still there by the time the police arrive, didn't bother to draw his gun.

When Prescott and his partner walked into the building, they met the three burglars walking out. All three had guns pointed at the officers, and Prescott had his shotgun pointing at them. The LAPD had a well-earned reputation for shooting whenever in doubt. That was what we were trained to do. Any seasoned LA cop would have pulled the trigger on that shotgun. The magnum rounds in that weapon would have cut the suspects in half before they even thought about pulling their triggers. The problem was, Prescott wasn't a seasoned officer; he was just a big kid right out of the academy.

Prescott froze but the burglars didn't. They ran straight into the two officers, knocking them backward, then ran into the night, taking Prescott's reputation with them. His partner reported that he was a coward, someone who froze in a fight. After that Prescott had to transfer to a low-crime division where no one knew his reputation. He is now working as an officer in a small town on the East Coast.

Courage Is the Outward Expression of Humility

Courage—or lack thereof—is often expressed when you haven't had time to consider all the angles of a situation. Had Prescott had time to evaluate the situation, including the possible outcomes, he may have made a different decision. Instead, his lack of courage was revealed in a moment of panic. By his failure to do what his training instructed him, the three burglars could easily have killed him and his partner.

The Bible is filled with stories of immense bravery: Moses leading millions of people into the desert with no water or food; David fighting Goliath; Gideon; Jeremiah; Esther; Abraham. The apostle Paul's life is one long saga of bravery and suffering. And at the core of courage is humility. Humility was the mark of each of these heroes' lives. There were some falters, especially with Abraham, but courage marked by humility was the overarching quality that each possessed.

Courage isn't something conjured up at the moment that it is needed. It is the expression of your character at a moment of testing. Courage is the sum of all your virtues expressed at a single moment in time. The person you have been, your secret thoughts, the skeletons in your closet, and a lifetime of training suddenly spill out. Would you run into a burning building to save a child with a crowd watching? What if no one is looking? What if you are rescuing an old man instead of a child? What if it is your enemy?

Near one of San Diego's best surfing spots, Solana Beach, a sixty-six-year-old man was training for a triathlon. He was just off Fletcher Cove and in a line with several swimmers when he exploded from the water, both legs in the mouth of a twelve-to-seventeen-foot great white shark. The man emerged long enough to scream that he was being attacked before being dragged under again. Despite the obvious danger, two swimmers in front of the man turned and swam back to him, into the growing cloud of blood where a monstrous shark lurked, and pulled the man through the surf 150 yards to shore. Sadly, he died a few minutes later.[10]

Courage is the expression of someone who sees something more valuable than herself.

Courage defends a victim by standing up to the bully, even though he's bigger.

Courage says grace aloud in a restaurant.

Courage witnesses to a stranger. A lack of humility says, "I don't want to ask that woman if she knows Jesus. I might look stupid." This is an attitude that values self more than another person's soul.

"Hang on. That's not fair! I don't really know how to share my faith," you might object. Then care enough to learn. Put down your pride and pick up a book by Greg Stier of Dare 2 Share. He'll teach you how.

Countless times I have seen my wife walk up to a stranger and say something brief and watched while the woman crumbles in tears. Elliette prays beside her for a long while, and then the woman hugs her tightly. I used to ask Elliette, "What was that all about?" "God just told me to go ask that woman if I could pray with her," she'd answer. "I hate it when He does that. I'm always terrified that I'll look stupid." Yet she obeys and lives are changed.

Courage isn't a lack of fear. It's being terrified and obeying anyway. Here we see why humility is the foundation of courage. True courage flows out of concern for others without regard to the risk to oneself.

Judging Courage

"The spiritual person, however, can evaluate everything, yet he himself cannot be evaluated by anyone" (1 Corinthians 2:15). Many Bible translations use the word *judge* where the word *evaluate* is used in this scripture. The English language has two meanings for the word *judge:* one is "evaluate"; the other is "condemn." People who don't follow Christ love to quote Jesus saying that we are not to judge (Matthew 7:1). Jesus means not to condemn. He isn't telling a godly person not to evaluate or discern.

How do we evaluate or judge true courage? Courage is an outward expression, but its true motivation is inward, and we can't observe that. As an example, let's take two platoon commanders in the same battle. Both charge a machine-gun nest, brave the bullets, and save their men. Each gets a medal for his actions.

The first man saw that the guns would soon mow down his men. He was drafted into the war; he didn't volunteer. He comes from a broken home with no father to teach him honor in battle. Terrified and without thinking, he charges to save his men's lives. He captures the guns, and his men live.

The second man is also terrified. He comes from a decorated military family. He joined the military because that's what all the men in his family do. He looks around for escape and sees none. He doesn't care about his men but is terrified to be branded as a coward. He'd never be able to look members of his family in the eye again. Seeing no way out of his predicament, he charges and his men are saved.

Are these men the same? We don't see their hearts; we see their actions. They each earned the military reward that is given by mere men, but God knows who they are on the inside, why they did what they did. "I, Yahweh, examine the mind, I test the heart to give to each according to his way, according to what his actions deserve" (Jeremiah 17:10).

One man says grace in a restaurant with meekness and humility out of pure gratitude to God, who gave him the meal. Another says grace to impress the people around him with how religious he is. He smacks of religious pride. Both have completed the same action, but one said grace in humility and the other in pride.

So how do we properly judge courage? We judge it only in ourselves. We can judge—evaluate—others only by their actions, because we can't truly know their motivations. And this is where the man of God must dwell—at a point of constant self-examination: *Why did I say that? Why did I react that way?*

Guard your heart and your integrity. Courage, or lack of it, is a window that reveals your level of humility, which makes it a primary signpost on your walk with Christ . . . and on your journey to becoming one of God's servant kings.

Chapter 10

GENEROSITY

You can easily judge the character of a man by how he
treats those who can do nothing for him.

—Malcolm S. Forbes

Therefore, brothers, by the mercies of God, I urge you to
present your bodies as a living sacrifice, holy and pleasing
to God; this is your spiritual worship. Do not be con-
formed to this age, but be transformed by the renewing
of your mind, so that you may discern what is the good,
pleasing, and perfect will of God.

—Romans 12:1–2

Many of the rivers in Oregon are cold and treacherous. When we were kids, our favorite river wound its way north along the eastern fringes of the Portland suburbs, through a thick forest of Douglas fir, spruce, and cedar. The river is deep and rocky, filled with crushing rapids. Its vicious undertows claim several lives a year. In other words, it's the perfect place for high-school boys to spend a hot summer afternoon.

There are several bridges that cross the river, where a kid can illegally jump into the icy waters fifty feet below. The problem with jumping from those bridges is that the torrential downpours of the Oregon winters cause the river to rise to a dangerous level. A swollen river turns powerful currents into a boulder-moving force. Where the river was ten feet deep the summer before, it may be only two feet deep the next spring, with a massive boulder freshly deposited just below the black surface.

On a hot day in early spring, a boy from our high school named Mark was the first to throw himself from a bridge. He hit a rock that hadn't been there before and was killed instantly. His parents prepared for the funeral and sent notice to our church and high school that everyone was welcome. My brother Frank wasn't going to attend the funeral. He wasn't going because he didn't know Mark. Frank was a two-time all-state running back, was ruggedly handsome, and is one of the most loving people I've ever known. Frank didn't just have friends; he had hordes of kids following him through the halls, hoping for his attention. Yet Frank often searched the cafeteria for any student, boy or girl, who was sitting alone and sat down across from him or her, bringing his fan club with him. He'd grill the person he'd just met with questions and spend time talking to him or her, extending friendship. When you became Frank Harrison's friend, you became everyone's friend.

Mark had been one of those kids. Frank didn't remember him but recognized his picture as someone he had spoken to once. Frank decided to go to the funeral because he wasn't sure how many kids would attend. Frank wanted to make sure a popular boy was there to honor Mark.

During the service, Mark's father read some excerpts from his son's diary, including a pointed section about Mark's rejection at high school and how a star football player had taken the time to talk to him and make him feel important. That moment had changed his life and made Mark a popular kid at school and the leader in the church youth group. Mark's father pointed at the square-jawed boy with the thick neck and bulging arms: "Frank Harrison was my son's best friend," he said.

Worship

This is the behavior of a servant king. What Frank did is generosity. Generosity is giving every aspect of yourself back to God, to whom it belongs: your money, your prayers, your time, your effort, your reputation . . . your rights. Worship is giving away all to God, and this is most often done by giving to His children.

The Scripture passage at the opening of this chapter says that when we worship properly, we'll be able to discern God's will. That's quite a promise.

The ultimate act of worship is generosity. We get the wrong idea about what worship is from churches that term the time of singing before the sermon "worship." Singing can be worship when we pour our hearts out before God in adoration and surrender. That certainly is a form of worship. But mindlessly mumbling lyrics to a song before a sermon is not worship; it is just mumbling lyrics.

So what is worship? Worship is generously and adoringly giving back to God what He has given us. Standing up before a sermon and using our voices to tell Him how much we love Him is nice. Seeking out ways to meet the needs of others and then sacrificing to meet those needs is awesome. That is the kind of worship about which God says, "You may discern what is the good, pleasing, and perfect will of God" (Romans 12:2).

God is many things to us. He is our creator, savior, master, judge. He is our very life . . . and He is our Father. When Jesus came to earth, our relationship with God changed to one of intimacy. Jesus said of those who obey Him that He no longer calls us slaves (John 15:15). It is no longer a master-and-slave relationship. It is the relationship of a Father with a beloved son or daughter.

In practicing generosity, it is very important to be wise about whom we give to. Avoid being manipulated by people or ministries. God has entrusted resources to you, and your giving them away is a holy act. No one has the right to demand what God has given you. You and only you are the steward of what God has entrusted to you. In humility, be generous but also be wise. Give to those truly in need or to ministries that are about God's business. Never give from compulsion or to get something back.

Generosity is the ultimate in trust because it says to God, "I know You will take care of me." When teaching your daughter how to swim, at some point you have her stand on the side of the pool and you hold your arms out and beseech her to jump to you. You have great joy when, in complete trust, she leaps from the safety of the pool deck and into your arms in the water. How sad it is, and how much joy is lost for daughter and father, if in fear she refuses to jump.

Generosity is jumping into God's arms. It gives great joy to both of you—and someone else gets blessed as well.

How Is Generosity a Symptom of Humility?

We saw from Frank's story that we can be generous in spirit—giving of ourselves and our time to benefit others. Generosity is humility because it says that we trust our heavenly Father to sustain us. It says that we understand that our daily subsistence doesn't come from us; it comes from Him, and therefore we readily give of what He has given us.

If we give away time or money, our level of generosity is measurable. Other types are not measurable, so how do we know whether we're truly generous in spirit?

I used to be late all the time. I didn't mean to be late. If I had to meet someone for lunch at noon and it was a fifteen-minute drive, I'd stand up from my desk at 11:45. It took five minutes to get to the parking lot, I'd inevitably be interrupted on the way out the door, and then I'd have to park and walk to the restaurant. But those facts just never seemed to make it into my planning. Consequently, I was perpetually fifteen minutes late. I would mumble a half-hearted apology and forget about it.

My wife, Elliette, pointed out how inconsiderate it was one day, and I somewhat defensively agreed with her: "I don't mean to be late, so what can I do?" Around that time I also began to feel the Lord's conviction that I had too much pride, so I prayed for humility. He taught it to me, and it began to show up in my actions.

At the beginning of a meeting years later, someone made the comment to a group that Harrison was early, and a few others chimed in, "Harrison's always early!" I just sat there stunned. Somewhere along the way, I went from someone who was always late to someone who was always early. After God taught me to have a much humbler spirit, the idea of making someone wait for me became unthinkable.

When I mentioned to my wife what had happened, she just smiled and said, "Ken, you've been early for years now." I didn't try to be on time more often. Instead, God broke me, and humility increased. Being on time was a by-product of a spirit that had matured in Christ. I have since realized that punctuality is a symptom of a generous spirit. Punctual people aren't always generous, and late people aren't always stingy, because culture and upbringing sometimes come into play. But it is a pretty good indicator.

We see in that experience that my sin wasn't being late; it was being arrogant. I simply valued my time more than the other person's. A humble spirit brought a change of thinking, resulting in a habit change to being early rather than late.

A Stingy Spirit

Just as generosity is a symptom of humility, a stingy spirit is a sign of arrogance and insecurity (which are often the same thing). A short temper, impatience, a judgmental attitude, envy, jealousy, and a divisive attitude all come from the lack of a generous spirit.

A short temper is triggered at what it sees as wasted time. Impatience fails to take the time to help another who may not have the same talent as you. Judgment keeps its watchful eye on others, impugning their motives. Envy and jealousy want things for self instead of being happy for others. A divisive attitude says that if you don't see things the same as I do, I will cast you out of the group.

All these things look to take from relationships, rather than to give. They are the opposite of generosity and are an affront to God. In effect, these attitudes and actions say, "Why does so-and-so have that and I don't? Why is he taller? Richer? Why does she get to have that job?"

Other People's Money

"If you are offering your gift on the altar, and there you remember that your brother has something against you, leave your gift there in front of the altar. First go and be reconciled with your brother, and then come and offer your gift" (Matthew 5:23–24). Generosity is giving what has been entrusted to you back to the Lord. It is not giving what is other people's back to the Lord. That is their decision. This applies to nothing more directly than to debt. If you owe your brother or sister and begin to feel the Holy Spirit stirring you to be generous, first pay off your debt. To give to the Lord while you owe someone else is not to give your money; it's to give the other person's.

I'm not talking about institutional debt, such as a home or car loan. Those are business transactions that you made with a bank or business, and they have a payback structure and timeline, which they agreed to. I am referring to money owed to an individual.

Leave your gift in front of the altar, go pay the person back, and then give your gift.

Forgiveness

"If you forgive people their wrongdoing, your heavenly Father will forgive you as well. But if you don't forgive people, your Father will not forgive your wrongdoing" (Matthew 6:14–15). Forgiveness is the ultimate in giving to others what God has given us. It is an act of worship with which our Father is pleased. To hold on to bitterness, resentment, and old wounds is to refuse to give away the forgiveness that Jesus gave us—the very basis of our salvation.

In many years of discipling men, I am amazed at how many are held back in life by resentment toward their fathers. We've already talked a lot about hurt. Hurt is real, but it takes only two forms: open wounds or scars.

It is time to forgive and turn that wound into a scar.

Chapter 11

MASCULINITY

A whole new generation of Christians has come up believing that it is possible to "accept" Christ without forsaking the world.

> —A. W. Tozer, "On Taking Too Much for Granted"

Evil people and impostors will become worse, deceiving and being deceived. But as for you, continue in what you have learned and firmly believed.

> —2 Timothy 3:13–14

M y partner Juan was a tall Argentinian who was a macho man in every sense. He had a wife and several girlfriends, even though adultery was a punishable offense in the LAPD. One of the sergeants had to tell Juan to ask his girlfriends to stop sending flowers and gifts to the front desk of the police station or they'd be forced to take disciplinary action.

I spoke to Juan often about Jesus. It was like talking to a wall. He nodded and agreed with everything I said, but I never seemed to get anywhere with him. He would insist that he was a Christian and that his obsession with women was just a little sin that he needed to overcome.

Juan always laughed. He loved life. On patrol one night, he introduced me to a beautiful German woman who barely spoke English. "I love this one, Ken," he said. "She has a little son. Two years old. I'll be a father to him."

"Juan," I said, "I'm thinking your wife might get in the way of that plan."

He frowned. "I'm a wicked man."

"You know what, man?" I said. "I don't even know what you mean by that."

"Yes, you do!" he said. "I must speak to you about Jesus."

We were driving up Vermont Avenue at about two in the morning. I was tired of talking to Juan about Jesus, but I told him to go ahead.

"No," he said, "I need a long time. I'm a wicked man, Ken, a wicked man. I sleep with so many women"—he snapped his fingers—"like that. They are nothing. I treat them as nothing, but they still love me." He grinned. "And I love them. I love them too much." It was hard to take him seriously. He loved to talk about Jesus but not in a real way. I think he believed that talking about Jesus was some sort of penance. There was nothing genuine in it. Juan was locked into a belief that if he just felt guilty and miserable enough about his sin, Jesus would somehow accept him.

"That's a lie, Juan," I told him over and over. "Jesus doesn't want you to feel guilty. He died to take your guilt away. He wants you to have a relationship with Him. He wants you to stop running around and be loyal to your wife. It isn't nearly as complicated as you make it."

Juan would nod as if he understood; then we'd have the same conversation in another couple of hours. I told him that God didn't want him to do anything; God wanted him—just him. No matter what I said, Juan was abandoned to the belief that he could keep up his lifestyle as long as he felt really bad about it. But the guilt was eating at him.

As I was trying to figure out how to get the truth about Jesus to him, a huge man leaped onto the hood of our car. He was screaming and blood was exploding from his head. In seconds the hood of our car was covered in blood. He was waving his arms in the bloody pool, as if he was trying to swim in it.

I sighed, stepped from the car and pushed his face up with my nightstick, and saw two things: he was completely high and his forehead was gone. It looked as if he'd been scalped from his eyebrows to the first inch of his hairline.

He was too far gone to realize that we were the police. His brain was registering nothing. He lunged at me, screaming and swinging his fists, so I kicked him in the chest and he fell backward into the gutter, unconscious. We handcuffed him, waited for the ambulance to arrive, and walked up to the motel he had just run from. A banner hung from the roof that said, "$28 per night/$6 per hour."

I pointed at the door leading to the motel office. "Well, there's his forehead," I said. The door was bulletproof, and there was a three-inch-wide window that was cracked and covered with skin, blood, and hair.

The Korean motel clerk opened the door and peered out at us. "Crazy man try to jump through window!" he screamed. "Window too small! I tell him 'No!' but he try to jump through. Stupid man. He say give him back his money or he kill me. I say 'No!'" We saw an open door and walked over to it. Inside was an obese prostitute lying on the bed. She was pasty white and covered with sores. A pornographic movie was playing on the television, which she ignored, looking bored. A coke pipe sat next to her.

"Are you with the guy who left his forehead on the office door?" I asked.

"Yeah."

"Yes sir," I corrected her.

"Oh, yes sir. Meanin' no disrespect an' all."

"What happened?" I asked.

She shrugged. "He got mad and lef' to go get his money back for the room. I told him that little guy in the office weren't gonna give him back his money, so he said he was gonna kill him and take it."

It was a usual story. He'd paid six dollars for the room, which was also the price of a rock of cocaine. When he ran out of coke, he got desperate and needed the money back for another hit. That's why the motel had a bulletproof door. "He was bleeding pretty badly," I said. "Did you try to help him?" She just shrugged.

We booked him at USC Medical Center's jail ward on the thirteenth floor. As they wheeled him away, handcuffed to his bed, I turned to Juan. "You want to grab breakfast and talk?"

Juan was sullen. "It's not enough time, Ken. I need a whole day with you to talk about Jesus."

I shook my head. "Juan, I'm getting married in a month, and I've got to find an apartment for my bride during these three days off we have."

"Can't you find her a place in two days and spend one day with me?" he asked.

He had desperation in his eyes. I don't know if it was because I was only twenty-three years old or because I was completely selfish or because I had grown so used to conversations with desperate people that I just didn't notice that he might have been genuine this time, but I was unmoved. "Tell you what, Juan," I answered. "I'll show up to roll call two hours early after our days off and we can talk then." That was the last time I saw him alive.

Three days later, I got to work early and lifted weights at the Rampart station gym with a couple of other officers. Juan never showed up. As we changed into our uniforms and walked into roll call, we were shocked to see our captain standing at the podium in a suit. Captains didn't come to roll call, especially at night, unless something really bad had happened.

Juan had driven down to Rosarito, Mexico, and shot himself in a hotel room, the captain announced. That wasn't the worst of it, though. He'd taken the beautiful German girl with him and killed her too. Somewhere there was a two-year-old boy orphaned by an LA cop—a macho, handsome LA cop.

Being a Man

We see in Juan a man dominated by lust and pride, which are the opposite of the humility, courage, and generosity that mark a servant king. There is a lot of bad information about what masculinity is in our society today. For the last two generations, the world taught us that a real man drank a lot, pushed down his emotions, and slept with many women. He was emotionless and impervious to hurt. He was the macho man, just like Juan.

After seeing the destruction that such teaching wreaked on society, the world now teaches a new message about men. It is convoluted and vague. It flees from machismo toward an equally dangerous lie; it teaches men to be effeminate.

Let's tear down the lie of society, which has come from the enemy of our souls, and look at what God says about masculinity. First, we must destroy the foundational lie upon which every other lie about society over the past several generations has been built: the lie of modern superiority. To do that, let's take a look at the greatest warrior who ever lived—Alexander the Great.

The Bible describes Alexander the Great as a leopard with four wings because of his ferocity and the speed with which his army moved (Daniel 7:6). It also describes him as a male goat filled with "savage fury," whose feet never touched the ground (8:5–8).

Alexander was indeed filled with savage fury, and his army moved with such speed that his enemies stood in horrified awe as he approached. As their spies reported how quickly he was approaching, some generals and kings went weak in the knees; others refused to believe it. No army could move that fast.

Alexander had one relentless goal, and that was to destroy King Darius III of Persia and be declared king of Asia. Alexander was known for being both horrifically cruel to his opponents and amazingly generous to his friends, but people didn't always know which they were. Many years after his death, one of his friends was seen to shudder when he walked by a statue of Alexander.

When he defeated Darius in their first battle at Issus, Alexander captured Darius's wife, mother, and daughters, though Darius escaped. The women were called before him, expecting to be raped and humiliated. Instead, Alexander pronounced that they would remain as queens and princesses and would be treated with dignity. When Darius's wife died a little while later, she was given a royal burial.

Though Darius still commanded a larger army, when he heard of Alexander's mercy, he wrote to Alexander, offering to divide the kingdom and pay a huge price for peace. One of Alexander's advisers, Parmenio, told him that if he were Alexander, he would take the offer. "So would I," said Alexander, "if I were Parmenio."[11]

Alexander pursued Darius, taking Persia from him as he went. The army continued to move with shocking speed and fury. Major cities simply opened their gates and begged for mercy as he came by, rather than risk fighting.[12]

Finally Darius staked out a place to fight. He had an army that Plutarch reported was a million men, though modern historians estimate the number to be between 90,000 and 250,000.[13] But Alexander's army routed the Persians again, despite being so severely outnumbered. When Darius escaped, Alexander pursued him in relentless fury. His army traveled thirty-eight miles a day for eleven days with little water. It's even more amazing when one considers that many soldiers were carrying their own armor, swords, shields, and javelins . . . and they were walking in sandals.

As the exhausted army rested one day, some Macedonians arrived with some water and filled a helmet for Alexander. As the king looked around at the drawn, dehydrated faces of his men, he handed the water back. "If I alone should drink, the rest will be out of heart," he said.[14]

As Alexander's army closed in, Darius's own men turned on Darius and ran him through with spears.[15] Alexander's soldiers found Darius still alive, lying in a pool of his own blood in his chariot. He spoke gratefully of Alexander's kindness to his family and said, "I give him my right hand." He shook the hand of one of the soldiers and died.[16]

Modern Arrogance

Why tell this story in a Christian book? Because there is a huge misconception today that modern people are bigger, stronger, and smarter than people of the past. This isn't true. The men of SEAL Team Six or Delta Force would find it very difficult to accomplish what Alexander's army did, and these were just his average soldiers. Consider Jacob wrestling an angel all night long (Genesis 32:24). Even the best wrestlers in the world today would have trouble doing that.

What the Chinese mathematicians, Egyptian astronomers, and Persian philosophers were able to accomplish without modern sources of information is astounding. Historical achievements like making precise calculations about the solar system without computers, inventing calculus, and understanding the existence of atoms without the use of microscopes are all incredible feats of intelligence.

We tend to read Scripture through a lens of modern arrogance, interpreting it using our "superior" intellect. We act as if the God who wrote the Bible and created the world and the very minds with which we reason needs our help in updating His dated ideas. We have become easily deceived by each new idea that comes along, and that tendency is pulling us from a foundation of biblical truth to devastating effect.

Why Does This Matter?

"God created man in His own image; He created him in the image of God; He created them male and female" (Genesis 1:27).

Satan has been around since before the human race, so he is playing the long game. Separating God's beloved children from Him is a marathon for Satan, not a sprint. His lies build on his lies until even people who love Jesus have assumptions they believe to be true that are not. His schemes last far longer than our short lifetimes. We seek passionately to avoid becoming pawns in his wicked game; therefore, we must understand his plans so that we can fight and defeat them.

Satan has been attacking gender, gender roles, and especially masculinity with a vengeance over the last few years, and even Christians have been deceived. Let's take a scalpel to the things that some of us may accept as truth that are not truth at all; rather, they are cancers that our enemy sowed in our minds when we weren't even aware.

Satan's scheme, now and forever, is to disrupt the two most foundational building blocks of society:
1. Our relationship with God
2. Our relationship with one another

First, there is something not right in us, and to make things right, we must throw ourselves on the grace of the Creator. A philosophical change that started centuries ago has spread across the world to convince people that there isn't actually anything wrong with them and, if there is, it isn't their fault. We are seeing Romans 1 play out before us now—not only are sin and perversity abounding, but people publicly commend those who live this way.

Second, this chapter is primarily concerned with our relationship with one another. There is nothing more foundational to who we are and how we relate to one another than the fact that God created us male and female. Humanity was created as two types—both are equally loved in God's eyes and both will have equal status in heaven. However, their relation to one another on earth is defined through distinctive roles determined by God at the foundation of creation.

The two genders, male and female, are together the earthly representation of who God is. Neither, on its own, is a full representation. This is one reason marriage between a man and a woman is so important and meaningful. The truest representation of God's nature is a healthy marriage between a fully masculine man and a fully feminine woman, each acting in submission to Christ and in submission to each other.

In recent years even strong Christians have often been deceived by the creeping blasphemy about gender that is now almost universally taught in public education. It is even taught in a growing number of Roman Catholic and Protestant colleges. Some Christians don't realize that some of their foundational beliefs about the roles of men and women have come straight from Satan.

What Is a Man?

"Be alert, stand firm in the faith, act like a man, be strong" (1 Corinthians 16:13). We will see in the next chapter that every man is to be a leader. This is why being proactive is the foundation of being a man. When something needs to be done, a man seeks to do it. He doesn't look around for someone else to accomplish the task. He doesn't make excuses. He doesn't complain, slander, or gossip. He chooses to make a difference where he is.

When we understand that a man is called to lead, we see that a hallmark of being a man is accountability. This is difficult for many men to accept, but you must recognize that you and only you are accountable for your walk with Christ, for your marriage, for the state of your children, for providing for your family, and for protecting your family and anyone else who may need it.

This does not mean everything is your fault; it means you are accountable for these things as much as possible. An unathletic man with great business skills may be better at providing for his family than at protecting them. An athletic man with less education may be better at protecting than providing, but each man uses what God has given him to serve in his capacity.

You are accountable for your marriage, but this doesn't mean it is your fault if it dissolves. The wife of a friend of mine began perpetually cheating on him. Despite all his efforts, she turned from the faith. As a godly man, he did everything he could to lead her back to Christ, but she left instead. Notice the difference between being at fault and being accountable. He did all he could in obedience to God, but she chose something else. Sadly, many people in the church blamed him. He didn't need to be blamed; he needed to be loved. As we will see in the next chapter, your job is to lead; your wife's is to follow. You are accountable for being the best leader you can be, but it is not your fault if you have been accountable to God and she chooses not to follow. Just keep loving her, as God has continued loving you.

The same can be said of your ability to provide for those in your charge—for your family if you are married, for the people for whom you're accountable if you're single. It isn't your fault if you have been laid off, but you are accountable for providing, whether that means finding another job, acquiring new skills, or taking a demotion—whatever it takes to fulfill your responsibility as a man. And we should never allow pride to get in the way of our responsibility.

Time

A Christian college did a study in which a student was put in a situation where another student obviously needed help. The study looked at commonalities of those who chose to help versus those who didn't. The result? Whether people helped or not was primarily dependent on whether they had time. Those who were in a hurry didn't help as much as those who didn't have much to do.

Talk to most men today and they will tell you how busy they are. A man who is busy is constantly running from one task to another. He has little time to consider his relationship with his wife or the nuances of the conversations he has with his kids. He certainly isn't listening for the still, small voice of the Holy Spirit, who is constantly giving him opportunities to be used for the kingdom.

Did you notice the pained look on the face of the girl who handed you your coffee? What a difference it would have made to her if you had smiled and said something nice. What if you did something really crazy and asked her what she needs prayer for? You'd be shocked by how many people can be brought to Christ with that simple question. Look past her face piercings and scowl and look into her heart. There's a wounded little girl wondering if someone cares.

In the LAPD, we were trained to be situationally aware. What was going on around us? Where might danger be lurking? Are you situationally aware for God's kingdom? Ensure that you have flexibility in your schedule that allows you to take time to see the world around you, to reflect on conversations you have had that day, to review your actions. You are a warrior in God's service claiming territory from the Enemy. There are brokenhearted people around you. Meet their needs.

Most men find that between work, the needs of their wives, and the demands of their children, they barely have time to relax. If this is you, you are accountable to find the time. Once you start the hard process of freeing up your schedule, you will find efficiencies you didn't know were there. You'll be surprised how much wasted time there is in your life. When you understand that you are accountable for being proactive about your own schedule, you will change it and life will get easier. Successful men know how to manage their time.

Destruction of Masculinity

"The cowards, unbelievers, vile, murderers, sexually immoral, sorcerers, idolaters, and all liars—their share will be in the lake that burns with fire and sulfur, which is the second death" (Revelation 21:8). The list in this verse describes the characteristics that God hates. This list doesn't mean that those who have committed these sins are condemned for all eternity, because Jesus came to forgive and free us from even these sins. The list doesn't say that someone who has committed a cowardly act is condemned. Instead, it refers to people whose lives are typified by these actions. Since Jesus's sacrifice covers all sins for those who have received Him (John 3:16–17), this verse is clearly saying that those who are typified by these actions are not truly saved.

The sins listed above are also a good outline of the fall of masculinity. I have found that there are four stages in the decline of masculinity. The sins are listed in order as a man cycles downward.

1. Passivity (Cowards and Unbelievers)

This is where many Christian men are today. They are good people, but they abdicate their responsibilities and roles. They obey the "rules" as best they can: they go to church on most Sundays and go to a Bible study sometimes. Their lives are typified not by action but by reaction. They don't work to improve the lives of those around them. Instead, they react to offenses, just trying to preserve what they have. They don't help that sad-eyed, face-pierced girl in the coffee shop. Instead, they sneer at her and judge her.

The passive man doesn't get involved. He is often obsessed with sports, golf, or even politics. He complains but does nothing. A sign of complacency is anger that comes from a feeling of hopelessness because he is unbelieving. He has no true faith in Jesus Christ.

2. Macho Man (Vile and Murderers)

This is the next step down. A macho man or a male chauvinist is someone who is insecure in his masculinity. He is constantly looking for ways to show or tell about his manliness. Of him the old cliché is true: "The older I get, the better I was."

He is a man of action but only action that comes from his pride. Say something offensive to the person next to him and he'll laugh. Say it to him and he'll punch you or insult you back. He is jealous for a name, but it isn't

God's or even those in his family (unless his pride is at stake). He is jealous for his own name because he worships himself. He looks down on the man in category 1, who is actually more masculine than he is.

3. Sexual Perversion and Greed (Sexually Immoral, Sorcerers, Idolaters)

This man is worse than the macho man. Machismo takes only enough to fill the hole inside an insecure person. The greedy and the perverted take more than the macho man, because greed and perversion actively destroy others.

The Bible says that greed is idolatry (Colossians 3:5). Greed can never be satisfied; therefore, it steals from others unceasingly. Consider the following verses from James 5: "Your silver and gold are corroded, and their corrosion will be a witness against you and will eat your flesh like fire. You stored up treasure in the last days! Look! The pay that you withheld from the workers who reaped your fields cries out, and the outcry of the harvesters has reached the ears of the Lord of Hosts" (verses 3–5).

Perversion is the opposite of caring for women and children. It uses others for one's personal gratification. The damage done to children who have been sexually abused can destroy their lives. The idea of emotionless sexual relationships is a lie. We see the damage done to people, especially women, all around us. First Corinthians 6:18 urges us to "run from sexual immorality!"

4. Complacency (Liars)

The next step down is complacency. This man is the complete coward. Lying is the twin of cowardice but is worse. Lying almost always comes from fear. A real man is dedicated to the truth no matter how difficult. It is amazing what a dedication to truth, no matter what, will do for your walk with Christ. If you refuse to lie to your wife about how much you lost gambling, you'll likely stop gambling. If you refuse to lie about lusting after other women, you're sure to be active in your resistance to such a sin.

A liar differs from a coward in that a coward is worried only about himself, whereas a liar wants to bring others along. The coward hides in the foxhole, refusing to fight. The liar does all he can to convince others there is no fight.

Let Us Be Men!

You may have read the list above and seen yourself. Revelation 21:8 may have scared you. If this list describes you, you should be scared. Be a man of action. If you are on that list, get on your knees, have an honest conversation with Jesus about who you are, and ask for His forgiveness. It's already there, waiting for you to claim it. Ask Him to fill you with the fullest measure of His Holy Spirit. Be honest and open because He stands waiting for you to run back to Him, just like the prodigal son's father (Luke 15:20). Ask Him to change you from the inside out and to take away your sin. He knows your heart. If your prayer is authentic, He will do it!

Let this be our calling card as men: "Pure and undefiled religion before our God and Father is this: to look after orphans and widows in their distress and to keep oneself unstained by the world" (James 1:27). No orphan or widow (meaning those in need and the oppressed) will ever be left wanting when you or I have the capacity to help. And we will hold one another accountable to teach others to do the same. Let's not just become servant kings. Let's help others to become them as well.

Chapter 12

MARRIAGE

A godly man lays down his life for his wife.

— Coach Bill McCartney

Husbands, love your wives, just as Christ loved the church and gave Himself for her.

— Ephesians 5:25

I n the early 1960s, Stan and Jessie Merrill were the perfect couple. They'd married just out of high school, got involved in church, and had two healthy sons. Everything was as it should be, except that the hearts of the husband and wife weren't aligned. Stan was in love with Jesus Christ. His wife was not.

When the boys were eight and ten, Jessie asked for a divorce. She started sleeping with numerous men, both married and single. Quickly her activities became known by their entire town. When Stan went to the grocery store, the boys saw men snickering at their father and women scowling behind his back. They felt humiliated and drew away from their father because they thought he was weak and a coward.

During the divorce Stan contested nothing, and Jessie took everything he owned. He was left living in a one-bedroom apartment, while almost every penny he made was sent to his family. When the divorce was finalized, Stan drove Jessie home—back to his old home—because she didn't have a ride. After dropping her off, despite knowing she had many boyfriends, he stopped to buy her flowers. At the shop he saw a figurine of two babies with boxing gloves on. One was lying on the ground with a black eye, while the other stood above him. Stan sent that and the flowers to Jessie with a note that said, "Down but not out."

Every Sunday Stan would go to where they lived and knock on the door. He wanted to take the boys to church, but most of the time they hid, and their mother, who was still sleeping, wouldn't answer. Stan would usually stand at the door for about half an hour, just in case his sons needed time to get ready. Every once in a while, Jessie would feel sorry for him and tell the boys to go with him.

This went on for four years until the younger son, Dewey, started junior high. One of the women at church had multiple questions for Dewey about his father: "Is he dating anyone? Does he want to start?"

When Dewey told his father about it, he replied, "That's nice, Dewey, but I'm not available to date."

"What's wrong with you?" Dewey asked. "Mom's gone. She doesn't love you anymore! She divorced you!"

Stan looked at his son with the gentle eyes of a man in love with Jesus. What Stan's sons had seen as weakness was just the opposite. Their father was a man of incredible strength who understood his responsibilities as a husband and father. "Dewey," he said, "your mother may have divorced me, but I didn't divorce your mother."

When Dewey told his mother what his father had said, she came to church with them the next Sunday. She was jealous that another woman was looking at him, and she couldn't believe what he'd said after how she'd humiliated him.

When the pastor saw Jessie that morning, he set his notes aside and preached on grace and forgiveness. He preached about how Christ forgives everyone who comes to Him in repentance. Jessie didn't wait for the end of the sermon. Halfway through, she ran to the front of the church and fell on her knees. Stan leaped from his seat and wrapped his arms around his wife while they wept together.

After a few minutes, the pastor called the organist over and had her play "Here Comes the Bride." He remarried them that day.

Jessie often struggled over the next forty years of their marriage. Dewey suspects she was probably bipolar, and her abrupt mood swings often caused problems for Stan. But she was fond of saying to anyone who would hear, "My husband never gave up on me, and he saved my life."

Dewey is a friend of mine, and he told that story to me many years later, just after he'd returned from his mother's funeral. "She was the godliest woman I ever knew," he said. "My mother led more people to Christ than I can count. She loved people; she prayed with people; she never stopped serving. She never forgot the grace that was shown to her."

The Purpose of Marriage

Then the LORD God said, "It is not good for the man to be alone. I will make a helper as his complement." So the LORD God formed out of the ground every wild animal and every bird of the sky, and brought each to the man to see what he would call it. And whatever the man called a living creature, that was its name. The man gave names to all the livestock, to the birds of the sky, and to every wild animal; but for the man no helper was found as his complement. So the LORD God caused a deep sleep to come over the man, and he slept. God took one of his ribs and closed the flesh at that place. Then the LORD God made the rib He had taken from the man into a woman and brought her to the man. And the man said:

> This one, at last, is bone of my bone
> and flesh of my flesh;
> this one will be called "woman,"
> for she was taken from man.

This is why a man leaves his father and mother and bonds with his wife, and they become one flesh. Both the man and his wife were naked, yet felt no shame. (Genesis 2:18–25)

God did not create man to be sufficient in himself. He needed complete fellowship with God to be whole, and he also needed complete fellowship with other people. The ultimate intimate relationship a man can have on this earth is with his wife, whom God calls his helper. We see that they are to be "one," a picture of how the Father, the Son, and the Holy Spirit are one. That is, they are to be in such complete unity that they are of one purpose and one spirit.

As we discussed earlier in this book, sin put division between us and God and between one another. In the human realm, this shows up no more blatantly than in marriage. We see division, betrayal, abuse, and deception so often in the marriages around us that the most common statement we hear about marriage is "Well, it's a lot of work."

If the two are one, it isn't work. But how do we get there?

How Do They Become "One Flesh"?

Here is a statement that might be difficult to accept: the only outward thing that separates biblical marriage from any other relationship is sex. Anyone can be roommates, share a bank account, raise kids together, and more. Sex is the action that causes the two to become one flesh. It is the ultimate unifier for two people walking in the way God designed. This act goes beyond the physical too. In actuality, it joins two spirits.

Consider the following verses: "Don't you know that anyone joined to a prostitute is one body with her? For Scripture says, The two will become one flesh. But anyone joined to the Lord is one spirit with Him. Run from sexual immorality! 'Every sin a person can commit is outside the body.' On the contrary, the person who is sexually immoral sins against his own body" (1 Corinthians 6:16–18). This is why sexual sin is placed in a separate category from other sins.

Any single woman having sex outside marriage in the time of Paul's writing would have been considered a prostitute. Paul wasn't referring to prostitutes as we think of them. Paul meant that any sex outside marriage is a grievous sin. This is because a sexually immoral person twists the most intimate act God created and turns it into cheap physical pleasure. Sex is designed to unite a husband and wife so closely that they become as one.

The message of the world has cheapened this incredible gift. As we grow in Christ and begin to see things through His eyes—seeing the way He sees—our perception of sex changes. We move from seeing sex simply as something we desire, a mind-set that leads us to think that lust is inevitable, to having an intense desire for only our wives.

Our Role as Leader

> As the church submits to Christ, so wives are to submit to their husbands in everything. Husbands, love your wives, just as Christ loved the church and gave Himself for her to make her holy, cleansing her with the washing of water by the word. He did this to present the church to Himself in splendor, without spot or wrinkle or anything like that, but holy and blameless. (Ephesians 5:24–27)

God gave man the role of leader of his family, but what does that look like? The world often tells us that leadership and authority are the same thing, but this is not so. Authority is that influence that the law gives to a police officer or a military commander. Authority says, "Sir, please exit the vehicle," or "Grab your backpack and sit down." Authority offers no reward for obedience, only punishment for disobedience.

We are not called to be in authority over our wives; rather, we are called to lead them. Leadership creates the space for a person to choose whether or not to follow. Notice that a woman is commanded to submit to her husband, not to obey him. I obey the commands of a police officer out of fear of punishment, but I don't submit to him. This is because submission involves equality and choice. Obedience involves a hierarchy and offers no choice. A slave obeys his master, and a child obeys his parents. But an equal chooses to submit or not, based on the value in the relationship.

Jesus always offers us a choice when it comes to submitting our lives to Him. Submitting to the perfect Leader maximizes our fellowship with Him and gives us ultimate joy as a result. In the same way, a wife chooses to submit to her husband or not. As husbands, it is not for us to judge her willingness to submit. It is for us to be the kind of leader to whom she can gladly submit.

We are not a perfect leader like Jesus. Therefore, it is incumbent on us to be as much like Him as we can be so that her choice is an easy one.

How Do We Lead?

"I want you to know that Christ is the head of every man, and the man is the head of the woman, and God is the head of Christ" (1 Corinthians 11:3). We seek to lead our families as Christ leads the church. How does He do this? He "gave Himself for her to make her holy . . . to present [her] to Himself in splendor, without spot or wrinkle or anything like that, but holy and blameless" (Ephesians 5:25–27). Someday Jesus will present all His children to the Father, having given everything, including His life by being tortured to death, for the purpose of presenting them without blemish. Whether they will be presented as such will be dependent on the level of their willing submission to Him. Similarly, we will be judged on how we present our wives to the Father. Did we give our lives for them, as Jesus did for the church?

Does your wife see in you the heart for her that Jesus has for His church? None of us will completely measure up, but the closer we get to this standard, the more oneness we'll have with our wives.

Going further, there are three overarching qualities that I've observed in great leaders:

1. **Vision**—All great leaders know and communicate who they are
   and where they are going, whether in an organization or else-
   where. Your wife must know that your relationship exists to
   glorify God. Leaders always keep themselves accountable to their

people and remain open to constructive criticism. Does your wife feel the freedom to express her opinion in a safe and loving relationship? Leaders are not defensive and they do not argue. Are your words leading to life and unity or to division and distress in your marriage?

2. **Ambition**—Great leaders focus on the health and growth of their organization (or family). From the moment they rise until they close their eyes at night, they relentlessly pursue the implementation of their vision. Does your wife see that you are seeking to present her to Christ "in splendor, without spot or wrinkle or anything like that, but holy and blameless"?

3. **Empathy**—Empathy is the ability to see things from the other person's perspective. There is no more important place for this than in our relationship with our wives.

Sex

A husband should fulfill his marital responsibility to his wife, and likewise a wife to her husband. A wife does not have the right over her own body, but her husband does. In the same way, a husband does not have the right over his own body, but his wife does. Do not deprive one another sexually—except when you agree for a time, to devote yourselves to prayer. Then come together again; otherwise, Satan may tempt you because of your lack of self-control. (1 Corinthians 7:3–5)

Scripture says that your body belongs to your wife and her body to you. We are not to withhold sex from each other. A man's body is a simple thing. Physically, we're pretty much content if we're fed, sleep enough, and have sex regularly. This is because our bodies don't dramatically change very often. The only significant physical change we ever go through is puberty—when we get bigger, stronger, faster, and start to notice the opposite sex.

Women's bodies are constantly changing. Even puberty can be stressful when they suddenly begin their menstrual cycle and the boys who were their friends start to look at them differently. Their bodies change every month. Pregnancy represents a massive physical and emotional change as motherhood can shift a woman's perspective in a myriad of ways. Then later in life, usually in their fifties, women go through what normally is the multiyear change of menopause that ends their ability to have children, an ability from which some women derive a large part of their identity—again, this is a major physical, emotional, and spiritual change.

As men, we must understand that pregnancy gives women a completely different way of viewing sex. For a woman, any sexual encounter can result in a life-altering event—pregnancy. For a man who is walking in the flesh, sex is primarily physical gratification and nothing more. However, for a woman, it is an emotional experience, and one encounter can change everything.

Men need to have certain needs met before we can have a sex drive. We must be healthy, fed, and warm, for instance. If you're starving, freezing, or sick, you won't have the desire for sex. Women need those same things, but in addition, they also need to feel safe, secure, and cherished. Your wife needs to feel that you would sacrifice your life for her safety, that you would give up everything you own for her company, that you would swim shark-infested waters to be with her. When a woman has this faith in her marriage and her husband, her sex drive is usually fairly congruent with his, unless other physical or emotional issues are involved.

We see the Bible come to life here. When a woman has the conviction that her husband is ambitious about presenting her to Christ "holy and blameless," she will respond to him with her whole being: physically, spiritually, mentally, and sexually. This is how God designed marriage.

Contentment

If your marriage doesn't look like this or if you haven't been this type of husband up until now, it will take time to gain the kind of trust that leads to respect. In order to build the foundation, you must increase and guard your contentment with your wife. She is your wife, and you must have no other object of your affection. She is your partner, and you have no other—not in your mind, not in your future, not on your computer. You must view no other woman as a possibility.

Unfortunately, many of us have been programmed to lust after other women from the time we hit puberty. The world's normal way of behaving is unacceptable for a disciple of Jesus Christ. Being content with your wife brings great joy to both of you. It will change how you speak to her, how you look at her, and how you look at other women. Great freedom comes when you learn to see women as sisters in Christ. A great change will come over you when you learn to desire your wife and *only her*.

If you've grown into a habit of lust, you're like most men, but you must learn to redirect this habit, because disciples aren't like most men. It will be difficult and you will fail. A habit is a habit only until you're aware of it—and then it's a choice. Be ambitious for your marriage, and be proactive in keeping your mind pure. Like anything else that is hard to do, it will become easier once you break the habit of lust. Satan will tempt you, throw images in front of you, give you reasons not to break the habit. But remember, "Resist the Devil, and he will flee from you" (James 4:7).

You may be thinking, *It simply isn't possible to cease lusting after other women.* I want you to know that it is absolutely possible.

Let's go back to our premise. The source of lust is an unhealthy focus on yourself. You will not stop lusting by simply trying not to lust. You will stop only when you die to yourself.

I truly hope you will hear me, my brother in Christ. Jesus gave us the key! The key is death to self, which results in discipleship and true relationship with Him. The sins that weigh you down will disappear, and life will become so much easier and filled with joy. Suddenly, having sex with a woman other than your wife becomes unthinkable—and your wife becomes so much more desirable as a result.

I used to sit on a board with a tall and thin older man named John Gordy. John was always crying. He had one of the most sensitive hearts I've ever seen.

Once, during a meeting, a board member started explaining the problem of high school and college girls who felt rejected and turned toward other women, becoming lesbians. John burst into tears, weeping uncontrollably for several minutes as his heart broke for these girls.

"We've got to pray for these girls!" he cried out.

A year or two later, John and I rode a train from Santa Barbara to Los Angeles, and I asked him about the ring he always wore. He told me that it was the 1957 Detroit Lions NFL championship ring. I didn't know he'd played in the NFL.

"I don't like to talk about it," he said. "I was a different man then."

As it turned out, John wasn't just a player; he was a notorious partier and was included in the book *Paper Lion* by George Plimpton and the movie based on his book. John told me that he drank a quart of gin per day and was so mean and angry that a college football player he coached once had told him that he quit football forever because of John.

John found himself drunk and suicidal one night long after his retirement from the NFL, and then, while watching a church service on TV, he gave his life to Christ. The result was the tenderhearted man I sat next to on the train who wept at the mention of sin. John saw no pleasure in sin—it broke his heart.

You can be the same as John. It won't come from trying to be like him or from feeling bad about your sin. It will come from dying to self.

Encouragement

Be an encourager of your wife. Do things that let her know you are thinking of her. Know the ways by which she feels loved and seek to show her that you love her.

My wife appreciates acts of service. She doesn't care about gifts or encouraging words, but she loves it if I take the time to understand what she needs and then do it. We often joke that my washing the dishes for her is the best foreplay she could ask for. Some women want presents; some need to be told often that you love them. Know what makes her happy and do it.

Do not be critical. Leaders build up and don't tear down. Your wife isn't perfect, and there will be times when you need to talk about difficult things. Do it in a way that builds her up and assures her that you love her. If she is immature and lashes out, avoid the need to defend yourself. Avoid the need to be right.

As you learn to communicate in a healthy way, she will learn to hear in a healthy way, but trust must be established if it has been violated by a critical spirit in the past. When your wife has things to say that are critical, learn to listen, take it in, and apologize. "I'm sorry" is remarkably powerful in a marriage, especially from a husband—because apologizing is usually difficult for most men.

Do not comment on how attractive other women are—not ever. Most men do not derive any part of their identity from their looks. However, many women do. Your wife needs to know that she is the one and only object of your attention and affection.

First Corinthians 16:13–14 says, "Be alert, stand firm in the faith, act like a man, be strong. Your every action must be done with love." Remember, Satan has two goals: he wants to separate us from God and from one another. There is no bigger victory for him than to create division in our marriages, because in this case he often gets a twofer. A man at odds with his wife will also experience struggles in his relationships with God and with other people. So remain alert and protect your marriage.

This Is Difficult

"Husbands, in the same way, live with your wives with an understanding of their weaker nature yet showing them honor as coheirs of the grace of life, so that your prayers will not be hindered" (1 Peter 3:7). Perhaps you think I've been unfair throughout this chapter. You may be thinking that I don't know your wife. "She is impossible, selfish, bossy, coldhearted, resentful, and quite possibly crazy," you might say. There's an old proverb that says a woman marries a man thinking she can change him and she can't, while a man marries a woman thinking she'll never change and she will.

But you chose her. At one time, you loved her so much, you said a vow that you would be hers forever. A leader is accountable for his choices, and you need to be accountable for yours. If your wife is no longer the woman she was when you married her, it is likely that you had something to do with the change. Notice that in the scripture above, our prayers can be hindered if we are not doing our duty to our wives the way we should. You will not and cannot be a man of prayer and therefore a true disciple if you do not honor your wife.

Your leadership is not based on your relationship with her—it is based on your relationship with Christ. I can't say enough that you will be judged by Christ on how you lead, not on how she follows. You must remain relentless in your pursuit of your marriage as long as she is willing to stay.

Divorce

Who can find a capable wife?
She is far more precious than jewels.
The heart of her husband trusts in her,
and he will not lack anything good.
She rewards him with good, not evil,
all the days of her life. (Proverbs 31:10–12)

Your marriage may be struggling. Your wife may have rejected your leadership. One of Satan's greatest tools is false guilt. He would rather you read this book and feel bad about the state you're in than read this book and do something to try to fix your marriage.

Stay focused on Jesus Christ. Do not focus on past failures, other than to learn from them. Do not worry about future failures, other than to plan for them. Stay focused on the present and on your responsibilities today as the leader of your marriage.

There are only two legitimate reasons for divorce: Matthew 5:32 provides an exception for sexual sin, and 1 Corinthians 7:10–16 talks about an unbeliever leaving the marriage. In neither case is it spoken of as a good thing, nor is it encouraged. In fact, the context of both passages clearly indicates that to keep the marriage intact is the far better choice, if you can do it.

God's opinion of divorce is summed up pretty clearly in Malachi 2:16: "'The man who hates and divorces his wife,' says the LORD, the God of Israel, 'does violence to the one he should protect'" (NIV). Marriage is precious in the eyes of our Father, and He holds you personally responsible to protect and lead your wife. Though there are rare circumstances in which divorce is allowed, they appear to be only when a spouse has completely quit the relationship. However, unless that point has come, a husband is not released from the responsibility of doing all he can to repair the marriage.

How our Lord leads His church is the template for how you are to lead your wife. Be the man God has called you to be and clear the space for her to be the woman God has called her to be.

Be her servant king and keep the emphasis on *servant*.

Chapter 13

THE FIGHT

Truth carries with it confrontation. Truth *demands*
confrontation; loving confrontation, but confrontation
nevertheless. If our reflex action is always accommoda-
tion regardless of the centrality of the truth involved,
there is something wrong.

—FRANCIS SCHAEFFER, *The Great Evangelical
   Disaster*

All those who want to live a godly life in Christ Jesus will
be persecuted. Evil people and impostors will become
worse, deceiving and being deceived. . . .

The time will come when they will not tolerate sound
doctrine, but according to their own desires, will multiply
teachers for themselves because they have an itch to hear
something new. They will turn away from hearing the
truth and will turn aside to myths.

—2 TIMOTHY 3:12–13; 4:3–4

S omething about hot nights in the LA ghetto just invited weirdness and crime. We wore midnight-blue wool uniforms (they looked black to me) with military pleats that were completely miserable when the temperature got above ninety. We'd reach under our uniforms and yank at the bulletproof vests that stuck to our chests through a sheen of sweat. The air-conditioning in the Chevy Caprice gave little relief. We kept the windows down, listening intently through the thick air for anyone who needed us. We also kept them down in case a bullet came screaming through the night. If it missed your head, you didn't want it shattering glass into your eyes. Such was Rampart Division in Los Angeles in the 1990s.

As I drove slowly down Alvarado Street, we saw what looked like a witch lurching her way down the sidewalk. Her face appeared to have blue icicles hanging from her nose and mouth. I got out of the car and blocked her path as she stared at me with wild eyes. Her hair stuck out in all directions, covered in white and blue paint. I could see fresh blood running down her legs.

When I tried to talk to her, she just hissed at me and tried to scratch me, as if she were a wild animal. Her mind was gone, and she'd obviously been recently and aggressively raped.

She couldn't speak but grunted and kept lunging at my partner, Duran, and me with long, jagged nails. She was clutching a brown lunch bag as if it were a prized possession. I wrested it away from her while she screamed and tried to attack me. Duran was holding her back and trying to stay away from her claws. The bag had two cans of spray paint. She'd been huffing—an expression for inhaling the fumes from spray paint—which gives a cheap high and kills brain cells rapidly.

We handcuffed her for our safety, but it was like trying to wrestle a wildcat. I saw a thick metal bracelet around her wrist with an address on it. We called an ambulance to meet us there and then drove her to the house, which was just a few blocks away. The house was one of the once-beautiful Victorian homes lining the streets around MacArthur Park. They were now drug houses or slums. A woman of about forty rushed out the door and grabbed the younger woman. She was crying and kept repeating the woman's name while she ushered her back to the house—and as my partner struggled to get the handcuffs off.

Inside the house I could see that the woman had done everything she could to make the dilapidated building a home. The sagging wood floors were covered with cheap throw rugs. The garage-sale furniture was arranged and clean. There were framed pictures of a happy family hanging on the walls. The woman looked over her shoulder at us as she wrapped blankets around the wretched individual. "I'm Naomi," she said.

Naomi didn't react to the blood on the woman's legs and dress—she was obviously used to it. She cleaned her face with a wet washcloth and rubbed her shoulders. I was repulsed, thinking, *I would never want to touch that filthy creature.* When Naomi turned around, her eyes were moist but there were only a few tears. It was the look of a woman who had cried herself out. They were tears of habit, with no other emotion. "She's my daughter," she said.

I suppose as you harden, you get better at covering your expression, but I wasn't there yet. She witnessed the shock on my face. I looked at Duran, who just stared at her stoically. She walked over to a framed picture of a nice-looking family—a mom (her), a dad, a cute girl of about sixteen, and a boy of about ten. She handed it to me. "That's her," she said. "That's my Michelle." I still remember her name because the song "My Michelle" by Guns N' Roses started going through my head, the song's disgusting lyrics painfully applicable to what we were seeing.

"That was a year ago or so," she said. "Her dad left about six months ago and took our son. We don't know where they are." She rubbed the girl's arm, looking at me out of tired, miserable eyes. "She started huffing right after that, just disappearing, and you guys find her and bring her back."

I understood the metal bracelet. With her mind so far gone, her mother had attached it to her so the police could find her home. I asked the only question I could think of. "Why don't you leave here? Why don't you move somewhere where they don't have all this stuff?"

"Where they don't have paint?" she asked. She'd been through this before. "I try to lock her up. I've tried everything. She's too strong. She beats me up. She always finds ways to escape. Then she goes off to that park . . . and she's there all night long." We both knew what she meant. She went there because someone would give her paint in return for sex. It would go on all night with her huffing away, oblivious.

The siren of an approaching ambulance wailed as it approached the house. Naomi cringed. "You called an ambulance?"

"She's been raped," Duran said.

"I can care for her," her mother replied. "I always do."

"That's not why we called them," he said. "We've got to collect evidence on the rape."

Naomi sighed. "Like you're going to catch them . . . No one cares," she said without emotion. And she was right. No one in her life did.

We are in a fight. If you don't feel like you're in a fight, then you aren't paying attention. There are misery and need all around us, and God has called us—as men who have received His gift of grace—to fight for His suffering people. People like Michelle and Naomi.

Colorado Springs is cynically referred to as the New Jerusalem by many people because of the huge number of Christian ministries there, including Promise Keepers. In 2016, thirty-six young people ages fifteen to twenty-four in Colorado Springs and the surrounding area killed themselves.[17] How could we have such an epidemic in one of the most Christian counties in America? Because these young people didn't see hope and now they're gone. But why didn't they see hope? What's going on? The apostle Paul told us a long time ago.

While Paul shivered in a stone cell awaiting his execution, he was thinking of us. God was showing him what life would look like in our generation, nearly two thousand years in the future. There he wrote down some warnings and some encouragement for us.

Paul had been betrayed and abandoned by most people he knew. According to church tradition, James and Peter had probably already been executed, and now it was his turn. He was a Roman citizen, so his death would be more merciful than others. He would be beheaded after he was beaten.[18] It was the penalty for any poor man who had ended up on the wrong side of Emperor Nero.

Paul had one last letter to write. As the Holy Spirit breathed words into him, he scratched a letter onto his parchment to his beloved protégé, Timothy. The letter wasn't just to Timothy; it was written to us too. Paul no longer had a scribe to help him write, so he carved out big letters because he was almost blind. He wrote with triumph, "I have fought the good fight, I have finished the race, I have kept the faith" (2 Timothy 4:7). Paul was looking back on a life of cold, starvation, torture, and repeated imprisonment (2 Corinthians 11:23–27). He had been hounded and hated and jeered. He was a good soldier of Jesus Christ, and death would come as a relief.

He'd written to the Philippians (1:21–26) that he yearned to die to be with Jesus but continued living to bring his brothers and sisters in Christ into deeper knowledge of the truth. Now the blind old man could go home, satisfied that he'd done all his Father had asked of him.

Paul sighed and waited for the cell door to open. He watched for the men who would drag him to his relief. The soldiers would laugh at him one last time as each blow came closer to releasing him from the prison of his body. Then he could finally see his beloved Jesus face to face for the first time since that day on the road to Damascus (Acts 9:1–9).

What did Paul say with his last words? He implored Timothy—and us— to hold firmly to God's Word (2 Timothy 3:14–16). And he offered the stern warnings that start this chapter. As we get closer to Christ's return, the following things will happen:

- Fake Christians (imposters) will increase (3:13).
- People will be more easily deceived (3:13).
- Most people will no longer tolerate what God's Word says. Instead, they'll listen to pastors and teachers who will tell them what they want to hear (4:3).
- Those who truly love Jesus and His Word will suffer at the hands of the deceived and the deceivers (3:12).

Do you see this happening around you? According to commonly held church tradition, Paul's fellow apostles were skinned alive, burned to death, sawed in two, and pulled apart by horses (Hebrews 11:37). They lived in poverty; they starved. These were the men chosen by Jesus. They were the ones to whom Jesus had said, "Count the cost!" Yet look at the teaching in some churches today. The pastor tells you that Jesus wants you to be the "best you can be!" He promises that if you just have faith, Jesus will make you successful. I wonder, then, what Paul and the other apostles were doing wrong.

When I was a boy, I had the honor of sitting under the teaching of a dear old missionary, Jacob Nordmo. After fifty years in China, he'd been kicked out by Communists under Mao and ended up retired at our church. In his thick Norwegian accent, he'd tell us stories of his days in China. His wrinkled face lit up when he spoke of God's goodness. He said that he'd prayed that God would give him a wife, so one day God told him to meet a ship in Shanghai and wait for a woman wearing a specific dress to disembark. While he was praying for a wife in China, a young woman in Minnesota, also called to be a missionary to China, was praying for a husband. God told her to board a ship for Shanghai and to wear a certain dress. As she was leaving the ship, young Jacob Nordmo walked up to her and said, "Excuse me, miss. I believe you are to be my wife."

"I know," she answered.

Their lives weren't a fairy tale. Just as the family was about to flee the Japanese invaders during World War II, one of their infant children died. Overcome with grief, Mrs. Nordmo clutched the corpse and wept while the enemy overran their residence. The family hid in some bushes, and so the Japanese soldiers wouldn't discover them, Mr. Nordmo gently but firmly held his hand against her mouth to muffle her sobs.

Mr. Nordmo's eyes twinkled with joy and he laughed heartily when he talked of Jesus. His prayers in public were memorable—often lasting for over an hour—and everyone could hear that a serious conversation was taking place. He knew God at a different level than others did. He was filled with joy, but his life was one of sickness, hunger, cold, and even the death of his children. Mr. Nordmo's life was the New Testament in real time. He suffered in many ways, yet he was utterly filled with joy.

Are you being persecuted? Have you suffered because you love our Father and refuse to compromise, or have you allowed the world to infiltrate your thinking? Are you being deceived, or do you stand solidly on God's Word and lead those in your care to do the same?

A continuing theme in Paul's writings is that we are soldiers in God's army. But soldiers fighting what? Paul wrote, "Our battle is not against flesh and blood, but against the rulers, against the authorities, against the world powers of this darkness, against the spiritual forces of evil in the heavens. This is why you must take up the full armor of God, so that you may be able to resist in the evil day, and having prepared everything, to take your stand" (Ephesians 6:12–13).

So we see that the deceivers and the deceived are really just tools of Satan and must be rescued from him. Most refuse to be rescued. Some just can't see the truth. Some love their sin and don't want to repent. Some just really love evil. If you stand firmly, gently, and humbly for Christ, people will have one of two responses: "To some we are an aroma of death leading to death, but to others, an aroma of life leading to life" (2 Corinthians 2:16).

The people who are angry and repulsed by the message of Christ are being genuine. They won't accept His grace, so they smell death when you come near. The godless are deceived by Satan. We must tell them the truth in grace and humility, and we must pray for them. But we must also protect others from their lies.

How Do We Fight?

The United States isn't the first country to accept the wicked practice of killing the unborn, an atrocity that we make tolerable by calling it abortion instead of murder. The Romans beat us to it. The Romans also accepted infanticide. Because girls could do little to support their families, they were seen as a problem. Romans would simply carry their female infants or disabled babies into the cold behind their houses and let the elements do their work. Christians, who understood the value and equality of all lives, searched along the lanes and alleys of the empire, listening for the soft cries of these suffering children. Among the children rescued were countless baby girls. They were raised and educated as equals with boys to become strong, intelligent women.

In a society where girls are killed, there is an obvious dearth of women. As Roman soldiers looked for wives, the church became a great place to find them. Warriors came to the church seeking a wife, and they found Jesus. Christian families formed and God's kingdom grew. Within a few hundred years, a small faith community had expanded and transformed Rome. Rome was conquered with love, not violence. It was conquered by the followers of Jesus Christ meeting the needs in front of them, not by angry people shouting down the evil all around them but doing nothing about it.

When the marines fought Japan in World War II, they didn't invade Japan directly. They took ground from the enemy in pieces. Brutal battles took place from little island to little island. Countless men died to win little rocks in the Pacific, far from the homeland of the Japanese. When one island was secure, they fought for the next rock. If any individual marine was to think of the strategy of the entire war, it would have been overwhelming. That's because the overall war strategy was left to the generals who were trained and gifted in such things. Each marine had to worry only about the battle he himself was fighting.

In a similar way, the spiritual war we're in is immense beyond our comprehension. When we see terrorists, abortion, sex scandals, greed, lying politicians, perversity, corrupt churches, child abuse, and racism, we wonder what we can possibly do. That is because Satan still rules this world, but Jesus is in charge of the war. He's already won, and now He's in the process of taking what is His—one "rock" at a time. We're not called to worry about the war; we're called to win the battle in front of us.

The deceivers, the deceived, and the just plain evil are all around you. They want to turn those you love into one of them. Guard your family; protect them from Satan's lies. Protect them from media, teachers, coaches, entertainers, advertisers, and employers who want to use them or teach them the world's empty doctrine.

Satan wants you to focus on the war instead of the battle in front of you. The war is exhausting. When we focus on the war, we watch Fox News or MSNBC and lament the state of the world. We argue about politics with our coworkers and sneer at the kid with all the tattoos. When we focus on our piece of the battle, we truly see the people in front of us. The kid with the tattoos may be completely in love with Christ. He or she may be the very partner you need to help bring others to Jesus. This person needs your acceptance, tolerance, and love, not your judgment. What can we do to bring our coworkers to Christ? How can we build up those around us? How can we listen to their hearts and pray with them and maybe even cry with them? The person you need to see may be your parent, your sibling, your child, or your girlfriend or wife. Listen to that person. Take the "rock" in front of you and trust your brother to take the one in front of him.

How? First, you must know God's Word. Start where you're at. If you don't know the Bible very well, don't waste time in shame; start reading it! How can you know what is worth fighting for until you know the truth? The truth is in God's Word. Anything that disagrees with it is a lie. Know it! Your family is depending on you to know your Father in heaven and His words so that you can guard them against the schemes of Satan (2 Corinthians 2:11). You may argue that you aren't an intellectual or much of a reader. Our Father knows you and what you're capable of—He will instruct you in His ways if you let Him meet you where you are.

What Do We Fight Against?

"The Spirit explicitly says that in later times some will depart from the faith, paying attention to deceitful spirits and the teachings of demons, through the hypocrisy of liars whose consciences are seared" (1 Timothy 4:1–2). An army is made up of soldiers with differing ranks. In a well-run army, a soldier's rank has to do with seniority and ability. The same is true in the army of God. Guarding your soul is for a private. Guarding your family is for a corporal. For a soldier of higher rank, though, comes the responsibility of looking past his home to others. A sergeant must be responsible for a small group of others in his care. Who? The ones God reveals to you. Start close to home. Your children have friends who visit your house. Ask them about their lives and their dreams. Listen to them. You may be the only man who ever took an interest in them.

After we were kicked out of the legalistic church I was raised in, I had the great privilege of attending a new church started by Stu Weber. An old friend of mine, General Jerry Boykin, is close friends with Stu, who lives in Oregon. Jerry lives in Virginia. One night Jerry and I were sitting around a fire in the Colorado mountains, telling stories to each other, when I asked him how Stu and he had become friends.

"I just called Stu one night," Jerry said. He drew on his cigar and watched the smoke drift away into the cold, dark air. "I wanted to tell him that I had read his book *Tender Warrior* a couple of years earlier. In it he says that if a man has the capacity, he should seek out boys being raised by single mothers and get involved in their lives.

"There was a boy down the street from me who I saw once in a while. I'd never seen his mother, and I'd learned he didn't have a father. I took him under my wing and taught him what I could.

"A long time later, he introduced me to his mother. Not long after that, she and I got married. Two years after I took to making an impact on that boy's life, I was his father! I had to call Stu and tell him that. We've been friends ever since." Jerry smiled into the dark, and I could see his face by the glowing ash on his cigar. He was a happy man.

Officers in the army are men who are responsible for many others. Too many Christians these days want to be officers without first being corporals. Jesus implored us to serve before we lead (Matthew 20:26). If you aren't guarding your family or the people close to you, you aren't worthy to lead a church. Paul said in 1 Timothy 3:5, "If anyone does not know how to manage his own household, how will he take care of God's church?"

Start at home. When the people you love the most love Christ and walk with Him, and not until that's the case, expand your circle. (To be clear, I am talking about leadership, not evangelism.) When you've made an impact on your neighborhood, perhaps God is calling you to leadership within the church. If you are married and believe you are being called but your family is not unified and following Christ, then you are lying to yourself. You may be being called, but it isn't by God.

The old quote is that you can judge a man by his friends. I think it's more accurate to judge a man by his enemies. We see from the Bible that a man who loves Jesus will have enemies (Matthew 10:18–25). If you don't have enemies, you probably don't stand for anything. I've heard it said, "The further a society drifts from the truth, the more it will hate those that speak it." A man of God in today's society will have enemies because he is standing for the truth. If you don't have people who dislike you because of your commitment to following God's Word, then you're probably not even in the fight.

My wife, Elliette, got a call not long ago from someone claiming to be with the IRS, stating that they were sending the police to arrest her and she needed to give them all her information to save herself. I've gotten that call; you may have gotten it too. When I got it, I just hung up. Not Elliette. "How could you do this?" she asked the caller. "Don't you know that these kinds of calls only deceive the elderly and the uneducated? How could you steal from such people?" The caller hung up.

Unfortunately for them, they hadn't called me; they'd called her and she's a fighter! She prayed against them and the damage they were doing to people, and then she felt a strong push to call them back. And she kept calling them. Each time, as soon as she explained why she was calling and began her lecture, the person on the other end hung up. Finally a supervisor answered the phone and yelled at her for interfering with their business. She cussed at Elliette and hung up. Elliette kept calling.

On the thirteenth call, a young man answered. This time, when she asked how he could do such a thing, he answered her, "Because I'm a wicked man."

"Why would you choose to be a wicked man?" she asked.

"I don't mean to be," he said, "but where I'm from there are no jobs. This is the only way I can make money."

"Do you know Jesus?" she asked.

"Yes, but He won't listen to me. I'm a wicked man."

"Jesus died for wicked people. He died for you," she told him. "He will listen to you if you repent of your sins and give your life to Him." Elliette walked him through the gospel and they prayed together. Elliette, like a marine in World War II, took the rock in front of her, and a young man on the other side of the world is on his way to heaven. Twelve other people rejected her or cussed at her, but she found the one whose heart God had been working on, and now he's saved.

In our fight, we mustn't concentrate on those who reject the truth; we must just keep pushing forward for those who will respond. We are commanded to love our enemies (Luke 6:27). And we see from examples in the

Bible that the more closely we follow Jesus, the more intensely the wicked will hate us. There was only one perfect man who ever lived, and they nailed Him to a cross. After that, they hunted down His apostles and murdered many of them too. It's worth pausing and asking yourself a very serious question: Who hates you and why?

Chapter 14

PRAYER

If you ask me, Is it an easy thing to get these communications from Heaven, and to understand them? I can give you the answer. It is easy to those who are in right fellowship with Heaven, and who understand the art of waiting upon God in prayer.

—Andrew Murray, *Absolute Surrender*

The urgent request of a righteous person is very powerful in its effect. Elijah was a man with a nature like ours; yet he prayed earnestly that it would not rain, and for three years and six months it did not rain on the land. Then he prayed again, and the sky gave rain and the land produced its fruit.

—James 5:16–18

As a man grows in Christ and becomes a servant king, he also becomes a prayer warrior. I can't think of a better example of a person who serves others through prayer than my wife, Elliette. She prays with women constantly. She prays late at night when someone needs help; she prays early in the morning with women who need her guidance; she prays in the hospital for people who are suffering.

Elliette prayed one day for a heroin and meth addict named Andrea. Elliette had prayed with Andrea's grandmother for a year that her granddaughter would come to Christ. Finally Andrea consented to meet Elliette. Andrea showed off the "Daughter of Satan" tattoo on her neck along with the satanic symbols tattooed on her arms and chest. Unimpressed, Elliette explained that God defeated Satan and was waiting with open arms for her to turn from the defeated master of this world and run to Him.

Elliette soon had Andrea and her boyfriend praying to receive Christ as their savior. Only a few days later, Andrea learned that she was pregnant. She was terrified because of all the drugs she had done and the damage that would have been done to the growing life inside her. She called Elliette and begged for money for an abortion. Elliette didn't give her the money. Instead, she gathered several women, and they prayed for Andrea and for her baby's life. I asked my men's prayer group to do the same.

Elliette asked Andrea to meet her, and she showed up with another addict, a friend from high school who was not the father. He insisted that Andrea must have the abortion. He explained that of their eight-person group of friends from high school, Andrea and he were the only two still living, only four years later. All were dead from suicide or overdoses. He didn't want to lose his last living friend.

Andrea and her friend raised the money for her abortion. She called Elliette and apologized for what she was about to do, as she was walking into Planned Parenthood.

We prayed. Inexplicably, Planned Parenthood turned her away. Our suspicion was that Andrea was too high on drugs at the time. Andrea made another appointment the next week and called Elliette as she walked into her appointment. "How could I not have an abortion?" she asked. She hadn't been able to stop her drugs. The baby was loaded with heroin and meth and would likely be disfigured and sickly.

We prayed.

While we were praying, the nurse prepped Andrea and gave her an ultrasound. The nurse left to get the doctor, and Andrea wept. The nurse never returned. No one came. After a very long time, Andrea got up from the table and walked out, making another appointment.

Andrea's next appointment for an abortion would require more money because she was nearing the twenty-six-week legal deadline. She struggled to save enough money, but a few days before the deadline, she had saved enough. On the day of her appointment, she headed to Planned Parenthood again. True to her pattern, on her way there Andrea called Elliette.

We prayed.

And that's when God met her. Suddenly Andrea had an overwhelming love for the life growing inside her. She panicked at what she had almost done and cried out to God that He would protect her baby from all the abuse she'd heaped on him. She called Elliette again and told her the news.

We prayed.

We prayed for Andrea's battle with the addiction, for the health of her little baby, for self-control during the rest of her pregnancy. A few months later, a completely healthy baby boy was born and is now being raised by Andrea's aunt, who is overjoyed. Andrea visits her son three times a week, the legal limit set by the state of Colorado while she tries to finish her cleaning up.

And we pray.

Prayer Is Worship

Several years ago when I was on a missionary trip to Africa, I arrived at an orphanage with a team of eight people. Our plan that day was to plant a few acres with sweet potatoes, cabbage, carrots, and other sustainable vegetables.

As I unloaded our trailer, eager to get on with a long day's work, about one hundred women met us and announced that we needed to "worship the Savior" before getting to work.

I waited impatiently while they sang incredible hymns for about forty minutes in beautiful harmonies that sounded strikingly like being in a black church in the US. When they were done, I started to get ready when they said, "Pastor! We aren't done worshipping yet." Then they prayed for us for almost an hour.

I kept thinking, *Don't these women know we have work to do? If we don't get going, we won't finish by dark.* Finally we got started. That day the project went so smoothly that we finished two hours early! It was a sweet time of work, and then we had time to play with the orphans for two hours. The kids were so hungry for affection that when I put my arms out to gather them in for a photo, they mobbed me, not letting go. We didn't get the photo, but I've never forgotten those desperate hugs of kids who just wanted to have a man hold them.

I learned some things that day: Prayer was worship, every bit as much as singing was. Prayer softened the ground and made the work sweet. Prayer gave us the time to remember why we were there. Prayer reminded me, as those kids insistently jockeyed for time in my lap, of how our Father in heaven wants us to be—*just kids desperate for time with Him.*

Dad

When the disciples asked Jesus how to pray, He said to pray like this: "Our Father in heaven" (Matthew 6:9). This was shocking to them. Nowhere in the Old Testament was God referred to as "Father" in such an intimate, personal way. Jesus was announcing a new time and a new way of relating to God— one where we would have an intimate relationship with the Creator, as intimate as a child with his father.

Where does Jesus tell us to pray? In our "private room" (verse 6). In other words, in a place where it is just us and our Dad—a personal, intimate place where we can seek Him and find Him.

God hides Himself from the carnal eye. If we are occupied with our thoughts and self-will, we will find little communion with Him. But for the person who withdraws from the cares of this world and earnestly seeks his Father, God reveals Himself and His will.

Doesn't this make sense? Is any other intimate relationship any different? If you are trying to talk to your friend but are distracted, thinking only of your cares and your agenda the entire time, will you find much closeness and quality communication with him? Do we expect God to be any less offended? Seek Him, put aside all other concerns, and you will find Him—and, with Him, the answers to all your other cares. Because He has the answers to them all anyway.

Prayer is where we learn to hear our Lord speak to us. Many people who are thought of as "strong Christians" and know the Bible well are critical of people who say they have "heard from God." I have found, without exception, that these "strong Christians" have weak prayer lives. The truth is that God draws near to us (James 4:8) when we are on our knees and speaks to us when we are submitted to Him.

As long as we hear the will of God only through others or reading a book or listening to worship songs, it has little direct power in and through us. When we enter into direct, focused communion with God—shutting out all other distractions—we learn to hear His voice. Now we can move forward with boldness and faith because our God—the maker of the universe—has spoken to us directly. Listening to God's voice means renouncing all our will and wisdom. It means destroying what we think we know and refusing to follow any voice except the Holy Spirit's, which becomes ever clearer as we become people who walk in the Spirit, praying continually.

Why Is Prayer So Hard?

In our natural state, we're constantly thinking about our flesh and the material world. We obsess over food, sports, social media, sleep, exercise, how we look, and so on. We are consumed with our decaying bodies and how comfortable they are. This is not where we'll find God.

In our fallen state, the soul is comfortable in this material world. This is why the Bible so often exhorts us to die to the flesh, which means our souls move away from the material world toward the spiritual world.

Apart from Christ, religious efforts are dominated by rules pertaining to the flesh: "Don't eat that; don't do that; don't go there!" This is why Paul sternly warned the Galatians against a religion of rules based on the material world, because it has the appearance of drawing us to God but actually has the opposite effect. God is Spirit, and we must learn to seek Him in His spiritual world, not in our material world.

"God is spirit, and those who worship Him must worship in spirit and truth" (John 4:24). Prayer requires us to move the soul into the spirit, which means away from the material world. If this sounds confusing to you, think of it as moving all your thoughts into prayer—completely shutting out the reality of your body and surroundings and thinking only of God.

I know this is unnatural to us, sort of like learning to swim. Like swimming, perseverance in prayer allows us to go from fighting the water to tolerating it—even seeking and enjoying it. Take a moment to read Romans 8 and consider the command that we are to walk according to the Spirit and not according to the flesh. Does this make more sense now? It is in our spirit that we find God, not in the material world, or the flesh.

To people dedicated to walking in the Spirit, prayer comes easily and naturally, and their lives are filled with power. To people dominated by the flesh, prayer comes awkwardly and with little power.

So how do we go beyond a drifting mind and awkward prayers? *Perseverance.*

Perseverance

He then told them a parable on the need for them to pray always and not become discouraged: "There was a judge in a certain town who didn't fear God or respect man. And a widow in that town kept coming to him, saying, 'Give me justice against my adversary.'

"For a while he was unwilling, but later he said to himself, 'Even though I don't fear God or respect man, yet because this widow keeps pestering me, I will give her justice, so she doesn't wear me out by her persistent coming.'"

Then the Lord said, "Listen to what the unjust judge says. Will not God grant justice to His elect who cry out to Him day and night? Will He delay to help them? I tell you that He will swiftly grant them justice. Nevertheless, when the Son of Man comes, will He find that faith on earth?" (Luke 18:1–8)

There is a famous quote by George W. Cecil that says, "On the Plains of Hesitation bleach the bones of countless millions who, at the Dawn of Victory, sat down to wait—and waiting, died."[19] That's what can happen to soldiers of Christ too. Praying with perseverance is the secret of the spiritual life.

A five-year-old boy says, "Dad, let me drive the tractor." His father says no because the boy isn't ready. At ten the boy again asks to drive the tractor, and his father says no. At fifteen he asks again, and his father, knowing that he now has the maturity to handle the responsibility, says yes. Had the boy not asked again to drive the tractor, his father might have forgotten and the blessing would never have been the boy's.

Our Father in heaven doesn't forget, of course, but He seeks to give us joy and fulfillment in every form. If we aren't passionate enough to keep coming to Him with our request, then, really, how important is it to us?

As fathers, we would assign our children only tasks that they had the maturity to accomplish. Would we expect God to act any differently? We want to do a great thing for Him, just like a small boy who pesters his father to let him do a chore far above his ability. As fathers we say no because we know what our children can handle. If we give them too much, they could be hurt. So, too, our Father gives us what we can handle.

Why is there a delay in His saying yes? Our immaturity isn't always the reason. Remember that we are in a battle "against the rulers, against the authorities, against the world powers of this darkness, against the spiritual forces of evil in the heavens" (Ephesians 6:12). There can be reasons far outside our awareness and understanding that keep the Lord from granting our request.

The great prophet Daniel did not get an answer because Satan was battling to prevent delivery of the message (Daniel 10:12–13). There is a spiritual battle we can't see that may prevent us from getting an answer we seek. Therefore, it is imperative that we never give up going to the King with our requests. We never know whether we've given up just before deliverance was at the door.

When we get down on our faces and seek our Lord in humility, perseverance, and faith, we in the Spirit leave this sin-enslaved world and enter His holy presence. When we have learned to pray, there are no drifting minds or thoughts of this world because we are in the presence of the King. We rest there and seek to come back as often as we can.

Sin

There is another reason you may not be getting an answer to your request. God might not even be listening to you.

What? Doesn't God anxiously wait for all people to pray to Him because He's so loving? No, He doesn't. The Bible is quite clear the Lord turns His head from people who are living in rebellion and known sin. Consider these verses:

> We know that God doesn't listen to sinners, but if anyone is God-fearing and does His will, He listens to him. (John 9:31)

> You ask and don't receive because you ask with wrong motives, so that you may spend it on your evil desires. (James 4:3)

> I will not be listening when they call out to Me at the time of their disaster. (Jeremiah 11:14)

> Husbands, in the same way, live with your wives with an understanding of their weaker nature yet showing them honor as coheirs of the grace of life, so that your prayers will not be hindered. (1 Peter 3:7)

You may have noticed that we saw the last verse, the one from 1 Peter about how we treat our wives, in the marriage chapter. If we do not treat them with honor as our coheirs in Christ, living within our responsibilities as men who are given stronger bodies, our prayers may be hindered. And this exhortation should carry over to how we treat *all* women.

When we seek the Lord, we must confess our sins before Him and carefully consider how we have treated women, especially our wives. Never forget that God truly is a loving God, but He is also a jealous God who doesn't share His children with sin (Exodus 34:14). He waits patiently for us to leave our sins behind and humbly confess them to Him. When we do, He will rush to us.

God, the great giver, delights to give things to us (Luke 12:32). But in the modern church we have swallowed a lie that implies we can sin as we please without consequence. Don't fall for that deception! Sin interrupts our fellowship with our heavenly Father, cutting us off from the source of life. This is where our terrible lack of joy comes from. Come humbly before the Lord and confess your sins and walk uprightly before Him and He will hear your prayers and delight to give you the desires of your heart (Psalm 37:4).

Chapter 15

WAIT

Certainty is the mark of a commonsense life: gracious
uncertainty is the mark of the spiritual life.

—OSWALD CHAMBERS, *My Utmost for His Highest*

Wait for the LORD;
be strong and courageous.
Wait for the LORD.

—PSALM 27:14

F or many men, patience is incredibly difficult. We want to solve the problem now. We want to rush forward and take on every obstacle. Yet God often says, "Just wait, my son." God misses every chance He gets to show up early, but He's never late. This is because for those of us who have yielded ourselves to be molded into servant kings, He knows that we must learn to do things in His time, not ours.

I have a picture as the wallpaper on my phone. It is of my older son, Hunter, leaping into the stands at the Pepsi Center in Denver to hug his mother in celebration of his victory at the Colorado high school state wrestling championship. He had just pinned a kid who was a huge favorite. It is one of the greatest moments of my life.

Hunter had been a very small kid who was bullied as a young boy. When he hit puberty, his body changed, and he became a muscular and strong kid. And he found wrestling—long after the age most successful wrestlers do. He started wrestling in the eighth grade, and at the end of the season, he broke his collarbone.

Hunter started his freshman year at a large Christian high school that is the dominant football powerhouse in Colorado. It was a tough road back as he recovered while playing JV football. In practice for the last football game of the season, Hunter broke his collarbone again. He had to miss his freshman year of wrestling.

He was devastated. He told his mother and me that he believed in God but didn't trust Him or like Him. How could God finally give him this athletic body, after years of being bullied, and then let him get hurt and miss the only thing he cared about? Hunter struggled mightily with his faith. My wife, with her usual zeal, poured herself out in prayer to the Lord, and she got only one word in return: *Wait.*

Wait for what? Our son's heart was broken. He sat in the stands at match after match, at one all-day Saturday tournament after another, defeated and miserable. *Why, Lord?* we asked. Hunter did the only thing he could. He lifted weights and sat through every practice and every match.

Hunter's coach, Tim Welch, sat next to him and shared Scripture. Tim, with hours of sitting next to Hunter, spoke life into him. As Hunter's collarbone healed, so did his soul. As he went into tenth grade, Hunter was in love with Jesus and became a spiritual leader in school.

His senior year Hunter made it to the state tournament. Despite a record of 37–3, he wasn't even projected to place. In his first match, with everyone expecting him to make an early exit, he completely destroyed one of the best wrestlers in the state. And then he launched himself into the stands and into his mother's arms in front of thirteen thousand people.

Wait, God had said. *I'm doing what you can't see. All you see is misery, but I play the long game, and I've got our boy sitting next to a man of God who is filling him with truth and life.*

Certainty

"The wind blows where it pleases, and you hear its sound, but you don't know where it comes from or where it is going. So it is with everyone born of the Spirit" (John 3:8).

Is there some pinnacle, some zenith of spiritual perfection? No. This is a dangerous idea, as we can begin to believe that some people have reached it and we can fall into worship of them rather than the Savior.

No one in Scripture ever reached the point of certainty concerning God's will. The only thing we can be certain of is our uncertainty if we are led by God's Spirit. A man following his flesh and his own wisdom can be certain—though it is false certainty. He charts his course, saves his money, and does what he wants. A man following the Lord never knows where he will be tomorrow. He seeks and follows the leading of the Spirit. He lives in the present. He listens for that gentle voice that, when obeyed, results in his humility.

Paul was often perplexed (2 Corinthians 4:8). Abraham and Moses stumbled in impatience (Genesis 16:1–4; Numbers 20:7–12). We must learn to wait for and seek God in every moment.

Sometimes we cry out to God that we'll do anything for Him, and He smiles and says, *Then just wait, son.* "Whoever is faithful in very little is also faithful in much, and whoever is unrighteous in very little is also unrighteous in much" (Luke 16:10).

We say, "God, use me to change the world!" But He knows we still have too much pride, too much confidence in self, too much love of this world, too much concern for what others think.

He says, *Do the little things that I place in front of you every day, and learn to hear Me when I tell you to do them; then we'll get to bigger things.*

We say, "Send me to Africa to feed the poor!"

He says, *Why not start with the boy down the street who doesn't have a father in the home? Obey Me in little things and I'll give you bigger things.*

Sometimes our waiting for God isn't waiting for Him at all. Instead, we are waiting for ourselves to gain the maturity that He needs us to have in order to bless us with what we ask.

I was in a meeting with a congressman recently, telling him about a future Promise Keepers event at the Dallas Cowboys stadium. He was thrilled and said, "We need this so badly! We've needed it for years. I wish God hadn't taken so long to do something!"

"Maybe it's my fault it took so long," I said.

"You just got involved," he said. "How could it be your fault?"

"Ephesians 2:10 says that God prepared the good works He wants us to do beforehand," I answered. "Perhaps He's been waiting for me to get to the level of maturity where He could use me all this time. Maybe we could have done this five years ago if I'd have been stronger in Christ back then."

Faith

When the servant of the man of God got up early and went out, he discovered an army with horses and chariots surrounding the city. So he asked Elisha, "Oh, my master, what are we to do?"

Elisha said, "Don't be afraid, for those who are with us outnumber those who are with them."

Then Elisha prayed, "LORD, please open his eyes and let him see." So the LORD opened the servant's eyes. He looked and saw that the mountain was covered with horses and chariots of fire all around Elisha. (2 Kings 6:15–17)

Why don't we pray more? Partly because it's hard and partly because we don't really believe that it will make a difference. We come to God as a chore instead of grasping the truth that if we have the faith, we can alter the course of history with an impassioned prayer, as we've been told time and again in Scripture.

Or have we lost our first love? We don't come to Him in joy, knowing He can hear us; we come to Him in obligation with dried-up prayers. So how do we fix this? How do we grow our faith? The disciples asked Jesus the same thing in Luke 17:5–10:

The apostles said to the Lord, "Increase our faith."

"If you have faith the size of a mustard seed," the Lord said, "you can say to this mulberry tree, 'Be uprooted and planted in the sea,' and it will obey you.

"Which one of you having a slave tending sheep or plowing will say to him when he comes in from the field, 'Come at once and sit down to eat'? Instead, will he not tell him, 'Prepare something for me to eat, get ready, and serve me while I eat and drink; later you can eat and drink'? Does he thank that slave because he did what was commanded? In the same way, when you have done all that you were commanded, you should say, 'We are good-for-nothing slaves; we've only done our duty.'"

What is our Lord's answer to how we can increase our faith? It is to work hard, not expecting a reward. Those who work diligently will increase their faith, allowing them to do more and more, to hear His voice, and to have a vibrant prayer life. This in turn allows them to obey as second nature. Then God can use them for great things.

Eventually they become so productive in the kingdom that our Lord says to them, "You are My friends if you do what I command you. I do not call you slaves anymore, because a slave doesn't know what his master is doing" (John 15:14–15). A man of faith does know what God is doing, because he has become God's friend. He has become a man of faith through obedience, and a primary area of obedience is prayer.

Faith is the foundation of the Christian life. It seeks to be filled with the source of life (God's Spirit), and it walks away from the foundation of the Fall (an insistence on knowledge). Faith says, "I will go before I know, resting in the voice of Christ." Faith depends not on what it sees, feels, or thinks but on what God says.

We must remember that whatever our work is—helping the poor, preaching, witnessing—the work is the Lord's to do. We are only to be empty vessels that He uses and fills as He requires. A lack of faith stems from our age-old sin—confidence in self.

Intercessory Prayer

There are two primary types of prayer: personal and intercessory. For most Christians, personal prayer occupies most of their time. Personal prayer is about ourselves and the people and things that are central to our lives. All prayer is good, and personal prayer is certainly blessed by our Lord (Philippians 4:6).

Intercessory prayer is about others. It's a heartfelt seeking of the Father in behalf of people who may or may not have anything to do with our personal lives at all. It is spiritual warfare. It seeks to be a blessing to the body of Christ with little or no interest in self. An immature child asks for himself. As a child matures, he asks for himself and for his sister too. When that child is fully mature and has been put in charge of his father's business, he asks for all that will bless his father's business. A son and coheir with Christ has no higher interest than his Father's kingdom.

We should all have a long list of people and situations we're praying for, and that list should grow daily. What do we pray for? First, when people ask you to pray for them, do you? Do you take an interest in them and their interests as much as you would your own? When they say "I have a job interview tomorrow" or "My niece is sick" or "My marriage is in trouble," do you seek the Lord's blessings for them? True disciples take note and diligently and perseveringly seek the Lord in others' behalf, asking whether there is some deeper truth about the matter that they should pray for as well.

Pray for your brothers and sisters in Christ that their knowledge of God will go deeper, that they'll be protected from Satan's lies, that God will protect their physical and spiritual health, that He will become ever clearer to them. Pray that they will be filled with God's presence and experience His blessings to the full, even if that elevates them to greater status than you.

Here's a great truth: if you learn to authentically pray in this way, others you are praying for never will be higher than you, because passionate, persistent intercessory prayer is the height of the Christian walk. It is here that you will find yourself walking consistently in God's will (though often never absolutely certain about His will until you look backward and realize you were step in step with Him all along). It is here that He begins to guide your prayers, telling you whom to pray for and what they need prayer for.

Here you'll find yourself fulfilling the words of Jesus in Luke 17, where the slave comes in from the field and still has to cook his master's dinner before he can finally rest (verses 7–8). What's the field? It's the world. When we're done serving people and we go home, we then seek the Lord before we serve ourselves.

Are you this person? Most of us are not. Here is the great news: Jesus seeks Christians who will be broken bread and poured-out wine for Him, and He never stops seeking. Repent and become a man of prayer. Do not try harder; do not wallow in guilt—that's the road back to a focus on self and failure.

All you need to do is empty yourself and repent. God desperately wants a deep relationship with you and will do all the work as long as you get out of His way. He has prepared good works beforehand for you to do and will give you the power to do them, if you seek Him and wait for Him.

Judging Ourselves

"The spiritual person, however, can evaluate everything, yet he himself cannot be evaluated by anyone" (1 Corinthians 2:15). We saw earlier that we have difficulty judging ourselves properly because pride is the great blinder. So how do we truly evaluate ourselves?

We can assess the condition of our own hearts by the quality of our prayer lives. A carnal Christian rarely prays. A "good Christian" prays, but they are mostly personal prayers that have limited faith and therefore limited power. A true disciple is a person of real prayer—a passionate crying out to the Lord for the advancement of His kingdom and everyone in it.

This type of prayer is the sign of a man who is truly in love with Jesus Christ.

It comes from humility, which then throws itself on the mercy of the Creator of all things and seeks His blessing. This humility, in awestruck wonder, realizes that the very Creator has said He will listen to His children who obey Him and enter His throne room with confidence (Hebrews 4:16) to plea for their brothers and sisters. And those prayers, coming from a pure and repentant heart, can alter history.

Chapter 16

THE JUDGE

The best "apology" for the gospel is to let the gospel out. . . . Preach Jesus Christ and him crucified. Let the Lion out, and see who will dare to approach him. The Lion of the tribe of Judah will soon drive away all his adversaries.

—Charles Spurgeon, "Christ and His Co-Workers," June 10, 1886

We must all appear before the tribunal of Christ, so that each may be repaid for what he has done in the body, whether good or worthless.

—2 Corinthians 5:10

n 1980 Fidel Castro emptied his prisons, and the United States accepted some terribly violent people. Many of those people made their way to Los Angeles and took over the MacArthur Park area. The once idyllic park and the beautiful Victorian homes that surrounded it declined into an awful place, overrun with violence and drugs.

For a few months I was assigned to a special car that worked just Mac-Arthur Park on morning watch, which was the shift from 10:00 p.m. until 6:45 a.m. The park was full of people who were so high on rock cocaine that they moved like zombies. As we drove around the park all night, my partner and I were surrounded by mindless creatures who were capable of anything in order to get their next hit. All night long we heard screams and gunshots. When the sun came up on many mornings, we'd see bodies filled with bullet holes or with cut throats.

MacArthur Park was positioned on Wilshire Boulevard, one of the major commuter streets leading into nearby downtown Los Angeles. The park had become such an embarrassment that the city leaders essentially made a deal with the felons that as long as they were out of the park by sunrise, the police would let them take it over in the early evening, once the commuter traffic was gone for the day. Each morning hundreds of people wandered mindlessly into the surrounding streets to collapse on lawns and in alleys, out of sight, until night came and they could resume their relentless search for drugs and crime.

From the start of morning watch until about four in the morning, when the crime finally started to die down, my partner and I rocketed from one horrific scene to another. Our nights were filled with the screams of sirens and people. But just as the crime started to ebb, we had to begin driving people from the park. Most went on their own because they wanted no part of the LAPD. But every morning there were ten to twenty stragglers who had become so inebriated that they couldn't wake up.

There is only one way to wake up someone in a highly intoxicated sleep, and that is to smack the bottom of her feet. I don't know why, but you can yell at, shake, and slap a person in that state to no effect, but one whack across the soles of her feet with a nightstick and she'll sit up as if she's been shocked.

A lot of officers got nicknames from the people we dealt with every day, and mine was Superman. It took only a few days before word was out around the park that you wanted to make sure not to fall asleep too close to dawn and get awakened by Superman.

Twenty years later, I had been in business for a long time, and the park and my nickname were far in the past. I moved the headquarters of my company from San Diego to Denver and soon began a Bible study for homeless men in our house every Saturday morning.

We had a house in a forested area in the foothills of the Rockies, so some local pastors brought vanloads of men from the streets of Denver up to our property to have coffee and doughnuts and smell the pines. A herd of elk or a mule deer often wandered by, giving the men a chance to experience the real Colorado. Most of them didn't care about me or my musings about there being "no condemnation . . . for those in Christ Jesus" (Romans 8:1), but I connected with a few of them.

One of the men who ignored me every Saturday was a Cuban named Carlos. He had a thick accent and ended every sentence with "man," but it sounded more like "mane."

One day I noticed he looked jaundiced. His eyes and skin were yellow, and he seemed distracted. "What's going on with you, Carlos? You okay?" I asked. "Your skin looks yellow."

"Yeah, mane," he said. "I got the liver cancer. I gonna die."

I asked how long he had to live. "I don't know, mane. I got the tests, but I don't know what they say, 'cause I got no way to get back to the hospital to get the results."

"How'd you get liver cancer, Carlos?" I asked.

He made a motion of injecting a syringe. "I like the heroin, you know, mane? I got . . . you know."

"AIDS? Hepatitis C?" I asked. He just nodded.

I picked Carlos up at a park in downtown Denver that Monday and drove him to the hospital to get his results. At first they wouldn't see him without an appointment, but I was used to dealing with hospitals. They soon took him away and told me to wait.

He came out after a couple of hours and looked at me with sad yellow eyes. "They say three months I die." I prayed with him, and he asked me to drop him off at the park where I'd picked him up.

When we got there, he didn't want to get out of the car and I didn't want to leave either. "Carlos," I said, "how'd you get here from Cuba?"

"Castro, he let me out of the jail and so I come to America."

"Where'd you go?" I asked. "Did you come to Denver?"

"No, mane. I come to Los Angeles."

"When was that?"

"I came in 1989 and I come to Denver in 1991."

"Where'd you live?"

"I stay in MacArthur Park like the other Cubans."

That got my attention. Carlos was a resident of the park during the same time I was a well-known fixture there. He didn't know my past, and I didn't want him to know. I asked how he ended up in Colorado.

"Mane, the cops in Los Angeles are too mean. They beat you up for nothing. There was one cop, really mean. They call him Superman. He always whack my feet and make me leave, so I go to Denver, where the cops are nicer."

How good is God? He wanted Carlos to have every opportunity to receive salvation. He wanted to connect me to my past, showing me how far I'd come and grown through Him. Who knew that twenty years later a faceless man from the park would be a weekly guest in my home?

Carlos didn't notice me smiling, and then he made an awful decision. "I don't come to your house no more, mane," he said. "I go die happy." He made a motion of injecting himself.

"You're going to go back to heroin, Carlos?" He nodded. "You don't have to, man," I said. "You've learned better than that. Why not give your life to Jesus here and now and trust Him? You can die in peace, knowing He's waiting for you."

Carlos shook his head. "Jesus no make me happy, mane." He made the injecting motion again. "That make me happy." Carlos got out and walked away. After that I'd stop by the park on some mornings to look for him. I saw him once a few weeks later in a pack of homeless people. His face was drawn and he had lost a lot of weight. He didn't have long to live.

"Carlos!" I yelled and motioned him over. He stared at me for a few moments, then shook his head and walked away.

Jesus

We can't save people. We can't choose for them. We can invite them into our homes, feed them, and teach them, but they may still reject the truth of God's Word. Our job is to love them and to be relentless and gracious in giving the truth, but only the Holy Spirit can change hearts. A servant king does all he can to lead others to the right decision in patience and love, but the choice to follow Jesus is their own.

As we offer people a true choice by giving them the truth about Jesus, it's imperative that we remember who Jesus really is. We tend to think of Him as He was in the Gospels, as the lamb that came to be slaughtered. But that isn't the last time we see Him in the Bible. Jesus came back to earth to show Himself to the apostle John on the island of Patmos, which we read about in the book of Revelation. When He came back, He announced to John who He is now—the Judge of the world.

John was the last of Jesus's apostles still alive. James, John's brother, was the first to be killed (Acts 12:2). Then Peter, John's friend, was crucified, just like Jesus. The rest were hunted down and tortured to death.

Despite incomprehensible torture, the authorities had not stamped out the message of Christ. His followers kept growing in number, no matter what the Roman government did. Even with John, now sixty years after they had killed Jesus, Christianity kept growing. The Christians had some sort of power. It went beyond the physical body that the Romans were so skilled at killing; these Christians had a stronger Spirit than the Romans.

The Romans had tried but failed to kill John, too, so they'd exiled him to a rock in the sea. Here he could write no more; he could teach no more. He would freeze and starve, and then he would be gone.

But John wasn't gone. He had learned the secret that Paul talked about in 2 Corinthians 1:4–5: "He comforts us in all our affliction. . . . For as the sufferings of Christ overflow to us, so through Christ our comfort also overflows."

John was worshipping, ignoring the pain in his flesh and seeking his Lord, when he heard a loud voice behind him (Revelation 1:10). He turned to see his beloved Lord. Jesus didn't look the way He had when John knew Him sixty years earlier. This wasn't the man John had argued with and tried to manipulate (Mark 10:35–38). Jesus was in His resurrected body in His new role—the Judge.

> I turned to see whose voice it was that spoke to me. When I turned I saw seven gold lampstands, and among the lampstands was One like the Son of Man, dressed in a long robe and with a gold sash wrapped around His chest. His head and hair were white like wool—white as snow—and His eyes like a fiery flame. His feet were like fine bronze

as it is fired in a furnace, and His voice like the sound of cascading waters. He had seven stars in His right hand; a sharp double-edged sword came from His mouth, and His face was shining like the sun at midday.

When I saw Him, I fell at His feet like a dead man. He laid His right hand on me and said, "Don't be afraid! I am the First and the Last, and the Living One. I was dead, but look—I am alive forever and ever, and I hold the keys of death and Hades. Therefore write what you have seen, what is, and what will take place after this. The secret of the seven stars you saw in My right hand and of the seven gold lampstands is this: The seven stars are the angels of the seven churches, and the seven lampstands are the seven churches." (Revelation 1:12–20)

This passage ties an incredible amount of Scripture together to show us the identity of the Savior, as well as to illuminate our relationship to Him. From many pulpits today, we hear preaching of a soft and loving Jesus, and He has those qualities, but if we see only the soft side of Jesus, then we have a limited understanding of His complete nature. He was the lamb slaughtered for our sins, but now He is the Judge. Revelation 2–3 are His pronouncements, warnings, and judgments for the church and for each believer. As good soldiers, we would be wise to pay close attention to these last words that our commander Jesus left with us.

Terror

On Patmos, John was so terrified at the sight of Jesus that he fell at His feet "like a dead man" (1:17). This is the same John who had walked with Jesus for three years. He camped with Him under the stars, ate with Him, rejoiced and mourned with Him. Upon seeing Jesus in His glorified body, though, John was completely stricken. This was a different Jesus from before, and the sight so terrified the great apostle that he fainted.

When people in the Bible saw an angel or Jesus in His supernatural state, they experienced extreme reverence or great fear. Abraham, Moses, Isaiah, Daniel, Mary, Paul, and the apostle John all saw angels or Jesus in His glorified state, and each of these great people had distinctive and awestruck reactions.

Be skeptical of people who say that an angel or Jesus has visited and spoken to them, especially if their reaction wasn't like what we observe in Scripture. Remember, arrogant people want to shrink their world. There is no greater way to shrink one's world than to believe that God would visit a person and the ensuing conversation would be as equals! If Jesus were to appear to someone, would that person's reaction be any different from the terror of John, who was Jesus's friend and confidant?

The Church

While Jesus was on earth, He judged the extent to which those who believed in Him received His teaching (John 5:22–23, 30). Great emphasis is placed on truly hearing in the book of Revelation, and special blessing is promised to those who hear and heed this prophecy (1:3). Fewer and fewer people will have ears to hear as the end of the church age approaches. If the Holy Spirit can truly get us to hear Him, He will show us an abundance of God's grace and power.

The seven churches addressed in the book of Revelation were actual churches of John's day but also are representative of the state of each believer. We know this because Philadelphia, which was highly commended, was promised that its members would not have to go through the great tribulation (3:10). Jesus knew that the actual Philadelphians would all die long before the tribulation started, so He was clearly talking to believers from a later day, when the tribulation would be reality—our day.

The churches of Philadelphia and Laodicea represent both the current state of the church and the hearts of individual believers in these last days in which we live. Laodicea is the predominant church, filled with lukewarm believers who live lives of complacency rather than passion and grace.

Philadelphia represents the true disciples. Let's look at these earnest warnings that Jesus came to earth to deliver.

Warning 1: Losing Our First Love

The church at Ephesus (first letter) was complimented greatly with only one correction (Revelation 2:1–7). The correction is vital to understand because it is from this error that all the others come. The Judge reproached them for leaving their first love.

Though Paul, writing the book of Ephesians thirty years earlier, had commended their faith and love (Ephesians 1:15), Jesus never mentioned their faith and condemned their loss of love. The Greek here for "first love" means "preeminent love." When we understand that God's chief aim is to build a bride for His beloved Son, we understand the significance of the church losing passion for the Bridegroom and allowing their love to grow mundane. No matter how excellent their qualities, leaving their first love—losing the burning desire to be the bride of Christ—left Jesus deeply grieved.

Jesus is looking for a bride who is passionately waiting for His return and actively seeking communion with Him, no matter how difficult the circumstances.

In ancient Israel, after a man was engaged, he would return to his father's house. There he would prepare a bridal suite for his wife. He did not return for her until the room was ready, and it sometimes took as long as a year. The bride did not know when he would come to get her. When he did return, it would be with a large party of friends and with blowing horns and a loud shout. The bride would rush to meet him, and the wedding festivities would start immediately, with the wedding banquet lasting several days. After the feast, he would take her home to the place he had prepared for her.[20]

Do the following familiar passages now make more sense?

> I am going away to prepare a place for you. If I go away and prepare a place for you, I will come back and receive you to Myself, so that where I am you may be also. (John 14:2–3)

The Lord Himself will descend from heaven with a shout, with the archangel's voice, and with the trumpet of God, and the dead in Christ will rise first. (1 Thessalonians 4:16)

Imagine the groom going away to build the most beautiful bridal suite he can for his beloved, only to hear reports that she was complacent about his return. Imagine if she seemed content in her own town and showed little enthusiasm for him. This is how Jesus sees Christians who are making their home here on earth.

Warning 2: Selling Out the Gospel

This warning to the church of Pergamum refers to teachers who compromise the pure teaching of the gospel for the sake of money (2 Peter 2:15; Jude verse 11; Numbers 22–24). They not only back away from teaching the entire message of Christ but also actually teach that compromise with the world is fine. The Judge was not talking in the book of Revelation about most pastors who earn a reasonable living while serving the church. The warning here is about people who make themselves rich off of teaching an incomplete gospel.

This church was located in a city where the residents were wealthy and well educated, and sadly, they were compromising with the world. The next step after allowing one's first love to die is a love of money, which leads to compromise and selling a watered-down gospel. The Judge spoke of Himself as the One with the double-edged sword (Revelation 2:12) because He wants to separate the bride from the world to which she has joined herself.

Warning 3: Tolerating Jezebel—Men Abdicating Spiritual Leadership to Women

"I have this against you: You tolerate the woman Jezebel, who calls herself a prophetess and teaches and deceives My slaves to commit sexual immorality and to eat meat sacrificed to idols" (Revelation 2:20). Who was Jezebel? She was a historical woman who was the wife of King Ahab of Israel and the daughter of the king of the Sidonians. She worshipped Baal (1 Kings 16:30–31) and was known as an incredibly wicked woman. Jezebel killed the prophets of God and stirred her husband the king to do evil (1 Kings 18:4; 21:25). She filled the land with witchcraft and prostitution (2 Kings 9:22). Jezebel usurped the authority of her weak husband, Ahab, and was the real leader of Israel. When Ahab died, she illegally took up the throne of Israel, while passive men did nothing, until God found a man of action, Jehu, who put her to death (verses 30–33).

Though all Christians are equal in God's eyes, God instituted leadership in three areas: marriage, church, and government. There are several offices within the church (Ephesians 4:11). For example, the gift of prophecy is clearly given to women, though the role of leadership is not. There are five female prophets mentioned in the Old Testament, including Isaiah's wife (Isaiah 8:3) and Miriam, Moses's sister (Exodus 15:20). Female prophets are mentioned in the New Testament as well (Luke 2:36; Acts 21:9).

However, women are forbidden to lead in marriage. When women seek to lead, it is caused by one of two things: a lack of their husbands leading or what can be called the spirit of Jezebel. Women who seek to lead due to a lack of male leadership often do so with pure hearts, because they see a leadership vacuum that must be filled. In these cases it is a rebuke to the men and a call for them to grow in Christ. These are not the women the Judge is talking about.

He is talking about women with the spirit of Jezebel and their male advocates, who can be said to have the spirit of Ahab. Jezebel sought to destroy homes and marriages, often through sexual sin and teaching discontentment, to both men and women, in their marriages. Jezebel's ears were open to Satan, who wanted to counter the natural order of how our Lord created things.

Jezebel did this with the full support of weak-spirited men who ignored God's instruction on the role of the husband in the leadership of his family. The words of the Judge are sobering and even scary. Jesus promised tribulation for the people who were fully committed to her (Revelation 2:22).

Warning 4: Demonstrating Hypocrisy

This comes from the letter to Sardis in Revelation 3:1–6. Jesus really dislikes hypocrites. In Matthew 24:45–51, He spoke of the Day of Judgment and said that He "will cut [the wicked slave] to pieces"—emphasizing again the Word of God as a sword—"and assign him a place with the hypocrites" (verse 51).

Once people depart from a persistent walk in the light, they will continually fall into greater error unless they repent. Likewise, the Sardis believers refused to repent of their toleration of false doctrine and allowed the hypocrites to take over their culture.

There were only two classes in Sardis: those who were truly saved—"a few people" (Revelation 3:4)—and a great number who had a reputation for being Christian but weren't true believers.

Warning 5: Becoming Lukewarm

"I know your works, that you are neither cold nor hot. I wish that you were cold or hot. So, because you are lukewarm, and neither hot nor cold, I am going to vomit you out of My mouth" (Revelation 3:15–16). These people were "lovers of pleasure rather than lovers of God" (2 Timothy 3:4). Laodicea reveled in her luxurious works and supposed wealth and self-sufficiency, but Jesus called her "wretched, pitiful, poor, blind, and naked" (Revelation 3:17). This church didn't know its true condition. There is not a single compliment for these people.

I believe Laodiceanism is the overwhelming state of the church in these last days. The Judge is standing at the door knocking. He is outside the door, making His final appeal to her. There is no hope of His being accepted by the greater assembly, but His appeal is to the individuals: "If anyone hears My voice and opens the door, I will come in to him" (Revelation 3:20). Only for the sake of those who might repent, the Lord delays spewing this church out of His mouth.

The Father is preparing a bride for His Son. The Son desires a bride that seeks Him with joy, that yearns to spend time with Him, that loves to gather with others and talk about the coming of the Groom, when they will be together forever, ruling conjointly. The people in warning 5 have descended to the point of not caring at all for the Groom. They do a few acts of basic obedience and pat themselves on the back, telling one another what good Christians they are. They live for themselves and do a righteous act here and there and then talk about how good it makes them feel.

Warnings

Notice that the warnings look like a marriage that is dissolving:

■ Loss of first love results in

■ compromising one's morals, or using the marriage for one's own comfort and profit—which results in

■ tolerating Jezebel—abdicating one's marriage responsibilities—which results in

■ hypocrisy—acting as if things are good and one is meeting expectations when doing the opposite—which results in

■ lukewarmness—no longer caring about the relationship and pretending that doing even a little of one's responsibilities is some great favor to the spouse

The last state is only about oneself with no concern for the spouse. How would you feel about a wife who was lukewarm? She didn't make an effort to speak to you unless she wanted something. She did no acts of service for you unless out of obligation. When she did even a basic task, she bragged to others about it and said that it made her feel so good. When others bad-mouthed you, she did nothing to counter because she was afraid of being unpopular. When she saw your children in need, she did nothing to help, unless it was to be seen. Would you want to "vomit her from your mouth"?

My brothers, we are in the last days, and the state of the church is that of Laodicea. Run from it! Run to Jesus! Build a relationship with Him by seeking Him in His Word, by seeking Him in prayer, and by seeking out His other children with an attitude of giving, not taking.

We have seen a list of dos so far in this book: do absolutely surrender to Christ; do change your worldview to align with Scripture; do be a man of action; do humble yourself; do separate from the world and its desires; do flee from Satan.

This entire chapter is a don't: don't let your first love die! Everything we've studied after Jesus's warning to the Ephesians is a progression from that sin. Stay passionate for Jesus! And how do we do so? The same way we stay passionate in our marriages: we continuously look to please our wives by talking to them, listening to them, seeking to meet their needs, and taking care of their children. This is what Jesus asks from us, and He promises that if we do so, we will be welcomed into heaven with His proclamation, "Well done!" Those who have lived as servant kings will receive rich rewards, both in this life and in heaven.

Chapter 17

LET US BE KINGS

This is God's universe, and He is doing things His way. You may think you have a better way, but you don't have a universe.

—J. Vernon McGee, *Ephesians*

The eyes of Yahweh roam throughout the earth to show Himself strong for those whose hearts are completely His.

—2 Chronicles 16:9

The Judge does not just have warnings; He promises rewards to the obedient as well. Like a father who loves his children, He warns in love and promises great rewards for obedience. He promises to make us kings, figuratively through a life of peace and joy in this age (John 14:27; 15:11) and literally in the age to come (2 Timothy 2:12; Revelation 20:4–6).

You may have failed miserably since you became a Christian. You may wonder whether you will ever get to the level of some of the great people of God you've heard of or maybe even known. You may think that because you've been a Christian for a long time and are still lukewarm, you'll never be a success spiritually.

We saw in "The Rock" chapter that Peter had to be broken before the throne of God before he could become fully yielded to Jesus. For some of us, it is one great moment of intense pain, like the one Peter went through, that breaks our cycle of failure from living in the flesh. For others, it is a series of moments. A good friend of mine, John Cundiff, used to say, "Every day in the school of life a lesson is taught, and that lesson is repeated until learned."

Brokenness

Earlier, in the chapter on humility, I told you about a great humbling that had to occur in me just after leaving the LAPD. That was a moment when God could really begin working in my soul, but there had to be another moment. There had to be a moment when God completely brought me to the end of myself—and I asked Him for it.

As we have talked about throughout this book, pride is an insidious disease from which we all suffer. It must be destroyed before we can really walk hand in hand with our Savior. If you look at your spiritual failures, even the fleshly failures like slandering others, sexual sin, or greed, you will see that pride is usually at the core, spurring on your flesh. Not serving and lifting up others stirs up so many sins. It is a lack of following God's words: "In humility, consider others as more important than yourselves" (Philippians 2:3).

In May 2008 I began realizing that I wasn't growing in my walk with God. I was spending time in Scripture and prayer, but it was as if I were treading water with weights around my ankles. I was keeping my head above water, but just barely. My prayers were stale and cold.

When I lived in San Diego, on most weekdays before going to work, I used to drive to surf at sunrise near our home on Moonlight Beach. I was a terrible surfer, so usually after an hour or so, I'd retreat, exhausted and cold, to my truck to watch the waves and pray. God met me there one day with a strong conviction to pray for humility.

I had sold a majority of my company two years earlier to a large Canadian company that owned forty-two other companies. I was now running my old company for the parent company. When we sold, I held back 5 percent of the company and sold it to the employees who'd been asking for the opportunity of ownership. My partners, who were all much older than me, became millionaires. I was pretty proud of myself, and that pride was becoming a festering wound in my soul.

Pride is always accompanied by anxiety because pride produces a false sense of accomplishment. Pride gives self the credit for what God did, causing people to experience undue stress as they try to hold on to things that they don't really grasp.

Several employees had told me how happy they were to be able to buy in. One had mortgaged his house to buy as much stock as possible. One had cashed in his 401(k), using his and his wife's entire retirement savings to buy stock. That was adventurous and made me feel more responsibility than I preferred, but I smiled when they told me and hoped the company could deliver.

God met me near the waves of the Pacific Ocean and shined a light into my soul. I didn't like what I saw. He showed me that His blessing and the wisdom He had given were the reasons for the success I was taking pride in. I repented for stealing His glory and assigning it to myself and then prayed for humility. I was hoping He would simply give it the way He had so graciously given me wisdom many years earlier. This time, however, He needed me to learn it in a way that would be permanent and that would bring with it great blessing.

Less than a week later, I got an urgent call from the CFO of the company that had bought us. He said that our company was massively in debt. I laughed and told him that I'd just reviewed the financials and that we had no debt and were showing a healthy profit. He apologized and hung up. A week later, he called with a different tone of voice. They had combed through our financials. Not only were we indeed in debt, but our revenue and profits were overstated. Without my knowledge we had been borrowing money from the parent company in huge chunks.

They initiated a full audit, and I learned that the accounting team, which had been keeping our books before the sale, didn't know how to do accounting according to Generally Accepted Accounting Principles (GAAP) standards, which is what the parent company wanted. Rather than admit they needed help and risk their jobs, the accountants had misreported our numbers for almost two years, borrowing money to cover themselves.

I had been growing the company, opening offices, and recruiting new people—thinking we had plenty of cash. I had approved every one of those requests to borrow money, never reviewing exactly what I was signing from the giant pile on my desk each day. We did an internal audit of our financials and platform, which also showed that the software we had spent millions on was not working. Our chief technology officer, not wanting to lose his job, had been sinking more and more money into a worthless platform that he had authorized. He was finally found out.

It was all my responsibility. I'd been so busy growing the company that I hadn't given proper oversight. I'd naively accepted financials and reports on technology without asking the tough questions that a leader should ask. A thirty-minute review of the financials would have revealed what was happening, but I hadn't done it.

The stock our employees had paid $189 per share for was now worth zero. It was an internal valuation, so none of them realized the true situation, nor would they—until they tried to sell their shares.

I replaced the accounting and technology teams, flew to Toronto, and offered my resignation to the chairman of the board. He leaned back in his chair, folded his arms, and said, "You created this mess, Harrison. You fix it."

I didn't want to fix it. I didn't know how to fix it. I wanted to crawl in a hole and never come out. Every time I flew to one of our offices, I looked at smiling employees, many of whom didn't know they were holding worthless stock.

God brought me to the end of myself that summer, and He left me there. For months I felt alone except for Satan, who gleefully whispered in my ear, *You were finally found out! You're just a cop from LA. You thought God gave you wisdom but He didn't. You just got lucky all these years, and now all the people who counted on you have been let down.*

Then the financial markets collapsed. In October 2008, I flew to Sydney, Australia, to advise several banks and funds there on their US holdings. I met with over thirty institutions, and people were in a major panic. They'd lost hundreds of millions of dollars of their investors' money and wanted me to help them figure out what to do. Most of the meetings were in ultraluxurious suites, sitting atop the highest buildings in Sydney. In one meeting, the leader of a major fund looked at me across the conference table and yelled, "You have no idea what it's like to have lost people's life savings"—he snapped his fingers—"like that!" I looked down over the Sydney skyline toward the Botanic Garden, where I took my walk each morning. *Yes, I do,* I thought.

It's a fifteen-hour flight from Sydney back to Los Angeles. There was a lot of time to think. It had been nearly six months since I learned of our debt, and I was no closer to a solution. I had no idea how we would recover, especially now that the markets were in free fall.

I had a distant memory that was about to become incredibly important. Several years earlier, I'd gotten a call from a woman who worked for a large government agency. She had a slow Texas drawl and said she had seen that I was taking a class in Los Angeles, two hours north of where I lived. She was flying in to take the class as well. She would be staying with her daughter in San Diego and was wondering if I could give her a ride each day. I really didn't want to drive a stranger four hours round trip every day for a week but didn't want to leave her stranded. I gave her the ride, the week went by, and I never thought about it again.

As the flight from Sydney landed in LA on that Friday morning, my voice mail was full. There were over ten urgent messages from a federal government agency. When I called, a woman answered with a panicked tone and said they'd been trying to reach me all week. There was a major contract that was about to be awarded, and the agency had been instructed to put it on hold until they got ahold of me. "We need to award this contract Monday, Mr. Harrison. It's urgent, but someone very high up has put the brakes on this until you've submitted a bid on the contract."

"Who is it?" I asked, but the woman had no information.

I mobilized a team to write a hundred-page contract submittal over the weekend, based on the little information we had been emailed. It seemed like a waste of time, but we needed any revenue we could get. We submitted the bid early Monday morning, and about an hour later, I got a call from a woman with a slow Texas drawl. "Do you remember me, Ken?" she asked.

I didn't.

"Well, I'd never forget you," she said. "You were so nice to give me that ride up to Los Angeles all those years ago. You saved my bacon. I was going through a hard time financially, and you made it all right.

"Well, I work for this federal agency and we have a major contract to give out. The United States government is going to be closing thousands of banks over the next few years because of this whole financial mess. We need a national company that can take charge of this whole thing and help us out. Well, I saw that you sold your company and were running this national company now, and I figured you were such a nice young man to me and all, you should have a chance to bid on this contract." She then described the contract in detail.

"Ma'am," I said, "from what you've described, this contract could be worth an incredible amount of money."

"Yes," she answered, "yes, it could. Now, the committee meets at one o'clock today and will decide on who gets awarded the contract. But . . . it's pretty much up to the chairman. Whatever the chairman decides is who the committee will choose."

"Ma'am," I said, "can I have the chairman's name and number so I can call him and see what I can do for our company to get this?"

"Why, Ken," she said, "you're talking to the chairman!"

At two o'clock that day, we were awarded the contract. Within a year, we had made so much money that all the debt had been paid. By the end of two years, representatives of the parent company called all the employees' stock because it had become so valuable and was still rising in value so quickly that they wanted to buy it out before it became too expensive.

"Humble yourselves before the Lord, and He will exalt you" (James 4:10).

God keeps His promises but almost never as quickly as we wish or in the way we think. I asked for humility and He answered. He brought me low, really low, and He left me there until my heart was ready to really understand. And then He elevated me.

There was something so sweet between the Lord and me in the years that followed. It was as if we had an inside joke. As the profits rolled in and stock value skyrocketed, as people all told me what a genius I was, only He and I knew that I had done absolutely nothing. God took a small act of kindness done many years before and turned it into a huge blessing.

We have a habit of seeing our heroes through the lens of their finished lives, but we must remember that it was a series of choices that led to their final destination that made them great. Walking with God is a long process of going from the sinful nature's pride and the need to know to a place of complete faith. We're all on that journey, and God wants to bring us each closer to Him. Sometimes it is through His gentle nudging as we read the Bible and pray. Sometimes, though, it takes a time of great pain because God must break us in some area so that we can really grow.

Reward

"The Son of Man is going to come with His angels in the glory of His Father, and then He will reward each according to what he has done" (Matthew 16:27).

Remember how we started this book? I observed that many Christians are living life as if it's a preseason NFL game. That's just how the enemy of our souls wants it. He doesn't want you to realize that it's the playoffs and the season is nearly over.

God wants us to snatch people from Satan's hands and deliver them to Him as our brothers and sisters in Christ. Your past failures mean nothing except for the opportunity to learn from them. Your past successes mean nothing except for the satisfaction of a job well done for your Father in heaven. God lives in the present. Your brothers and sisters need you to be present. The suffering and the lost need you right now.

To those who belong to Him, Jesus is returning to take us home and to reward us for the things we have done after being saved. Our sins He remembers no more, but our deeds are precious to Him. So let us do the work that God gave us. Let us get busy. Let us be men.

Let us be servant kings.

Acknowledgments

I want to thank Dr. Joseph (Jody) Dillow for his incredible knowledge of church history, Greek, and Scripture. All the hours he spent studying in the University of Cambridge library were a huge blessing in the writing of this book.

I'd also like to thank some people who have been great spiritual mentors: Steve Brown at Key Life ministries, thank you for teaching me how to forgive the Pharisees! Stu Weber, thank you for teaching me boldness. Coach Bill McCartney, thank you for encouraging me to preach the Word. Dr. Raleigh Washington, thank you for teaching me to see other perspectives. Colin Millar, my dear South African brother, thank you for teaching me to pray. My mom and dad, thank you for instilling a love of God's Word in me as a young man. My father-in-law, Andre' Iseli, thank you for your constant prayers; they have been more valuable than you know.

A special thanks to Judge Vance Day. He is the face of modern-day persecution. He never stopped smiling and never said a critical word about anyone. Judge, you are an encouragement to believers everywhere.

I'd also like to thank the Multnomah team. What an incredible group of professionals—you made me look far smarter than I am!

Notes

1. Joseph Dillow, *Final Destiny: The Future Reign of the Servant Kings,* rev. ed. (The Woodlands, TX: Grace Theology Press, 2016), 969–71; see also Eric Sauer, *In the Arena of Faith: A Call to a Consecrated Life* (Grand Rapids, MI: Eerdmans, 1955).
2. Terry W. Glaspey, *Not a Tame Lion: The Spiritual Legacy of C. S. Lewis* (Nashville: Cumberland House, 1996), 104.
3. George MacDonald, quoted in "Be Not Entangled Again in a Yoke of Bondage," *The British Friend* (1892): 157.
4. Andrew Murray, *The Indwelling Spirit: The Work of the Holy Spirit in the Life of the Believer* (Minneapolis: Bethany, 2006), 32–33.
5. Mark Malek et al., "Implementing Opt-Out Programs at Los Angeles County Jail: A Gateway to Novel Research and Interventions," *Journal of Correctional Health Care* 17, no. 1 (January 2011), 69–76, www.ncbi.nlm.nih.gov/pmc/articles/PMC3154702/.
6. "Richard Ramirez Biography," Biography.com, last modified November 1, 2017, www.biography.com/people/richard-ramirez-12385163.
7. Murray, *Indwelling Spirit,* 83.
8. G. K. Chesterton, *Orthodoxy* (Chicago: Moody, 2009), 35–36.
9. Anonymous, "Compassion Is in the Eyes," in Brian Cavanaugh, *Fresh Packet of Sower's Seeds: Third Planting* (Mahwah, NJ: Paulist, 1994), 41–42.
10. "Swim Was Regular Outing for Shark Bite Victim," *NBC News,* April 25, 2008, www.nbcnews.com/id/24313314/ns/us_news-life/t/swim-was-regular-outing-shark-bite-victim/#.W2yRwthKiT9.
11. Plutarch, *The Life of Alexander the Great,* ed. Arthur Hugh Clough, trans. John Dryden (New York: The Modern Library, 2004), 44.

12. Donald L. Wasson, "Battle of Gaugamela," Ancient History Encyclopedia, February 27, 2012, www.ancient.eu/Battle_of_Gaugamela/.

13. "The Battle of Gaugamela, 331 BCE," Ancient History Encyclopedia, January 18, 2012, www.ancient.eu/article/108/the-battle-of-gaugamela-331-bce/.

14. Plutarch, *Life of Alexander the Great*, 44.

15. Jacob Abbott, *Alexander the Great* (New York: Harper & Brothers, 1902), 225.

16. Plutarch, *Life of Alexander the Great*, 44.

17. Jennifer Brown, "Four Colorado Counties with Highest Rates of Youth Suicide Focus of Suicide Prevention Initiatives," *Denver Post*, December 12, 2017, www.denverpost.com/2017/12/12/colorado-counties-with-highest-youth-suicide-rates/.

18. John Pollock, *The Apostle: A Life of Paul*, rev. ed. (Colorado Springs, CO: David C Cook, 2012), 298.

19. George W. Cecil, quoted in Suzy Platt, ed., *Respectfully Quoted: A Dictionary of Quotations* (New York: Barnes and Noble, 1993), 342.

20. Dillow, *Final Destiny*, 814–15.

P.S. —

If you're ready to take the next step as a servant king, I'm inviting you to lock arms with millions of other men of God who will follow Christ into today's broken world to change our families, churches, and communities.

We are launching the new era of Promise Keepers because our nation needs men of God more than ever.

Join with other Promise Keepers across our nation to help drive our movement of change-making men. Learn more at PromiseKeepers.org.
You'll never be the same.

Ken

Now More Than Ever . . .

It's time for a new movement of men. Let's become who we're created to **be**, knowing our identity, purpose, and destiny in Christ. Then let's **do**, linking arms to change the world for good. That's why we're launching the new era of Promise Keepers. We're inviting you to join with us.

Next Action Steps: 4 Ways You Can Make This Real

1 – **Join our Facebook group page** to discuss this book with other like-minded men and interact with the author through weekly chats. Go to www.facebook.com/groups/ServantKings.

2 – **Visit RiseoftheServantKings.org** for additional behind-the-scenes content (like why Ken wrote this book), Q/A with the author, and download extra resources for you and your church.

3 – **Visit PromiseKeepers.org** to join the movement and learn how you can get involved with other guys in your community.

4 – **Call men together** to watch the 2020 Promise Keepers event live from AT&T Stadium, home of the Dallas Cowboys, July 31–August 1, 2020.

Men, we're here for you. We're all in this together. Together, we can change our families, our churches, and our communities for Christ.

Let's Make Our Lives Count